Walking in Their Sandals

Walking in Their Sandals
A Guide to First-Century Israelite Ethnic Identity

MARKUS CROMHOUT

CASCADE *Books* • Eugene, Oregon

WALKING IN THEIR SANDALS
A Guide to First-Century Israelite Ethnic Identity

Copyright © 2010 Markus Cromhout. All rights reserved. Except for brief quotations in critical publications or reviews, no part of this book may be reproduced in any manner without prior written permission from the publisher. Write: Permissions, Wipf and Stock Publishers, 199 W. 8th Ave., Suite 3, Eugene, OR 97401.

Cascade Books
An Imprint of Wipf and Stock Publishers
199 W. 8th Ave., Suite 3
Eugene, OR 97401

www.wipfandstock.com

ISBN 13: 978-1-60608-649-0

Cataloging-in-Publication data:

Cromhout, Markus.

    Walking in their sandals : a guide to first-century Israelite ethnic identity / Markus Cromhout.

    xvi + 128 p. ; 23 cm. — Includes bibliographical references and index.

    ISBN 13: 978-1-60608-649-0

    1. Ethnicity—Biblical teaching. 2. Bible. N.T. Gospels—Criticism, interpretation, etc. 3. Paul, the Apostle, Saint—Criticism, interpretation, etc. 4. Bible. N.T. Epistles of Paul—Criticism, interpretation, etc. I. Title.

BS2555.2 C75 2010

Manufactured in the U.S.A.

*For my family, Joy, Maxine, and Jessica,
and for my parents*

Contents

Abbreviations • *ix*

Introduction • *xiii*

1 An Introduction to Ethnicity Theory • 1

2 A Socio-Cultural Model of Israelite Ethnicity • 35

3 What Advantage Is There in Being a Judean? A Conversation with the New Perspective on Paul • 73

Bibliography • 107

Index of Ancient Documents • 115

Index of Subjects • 127

Abbreviations

APOCRYPHA

2 Ezra	2 Ezra
4 Ezra	4 Ezra
Tob	Tobit
Jdt	Judith
AddEsth	Additions to Esther
WisSol	Wisdom of Solomon
Sir	Sirach
1 Bar	1 Baruch
LetJer	Letter of Jeremiah
PrAzar	Prayer of Azariah
Sus	Susanna
Bel	Bel and the Dragon
1 Macc	1 Maccabees
2 Macc	2 Maccabees

PSEUDEPIGRAPHA

2 Bar.	2 (Syriac) Baruch
1 En.	1 (Ethiopic) Enoch
2 En.	2 (Slavonic) Enoch
T. Job	Testament of Job
Jos. Asen.	Joseph and Asenath
Jub.	Jubilees
Let. Aris.	Letter of Aristeas
L.A.B.	Liber antiquitatum biblicarum
3 Macc	3 Maccabees
4 Macc	4 Maccabees
T. Mos.	Testament of Moses
Liv. Pro.	Lives of the Prophets
Sib. Or.	Sibylline Oracles
Pss. Sol.	Psalms of Solomon

Abbreviations

T. Sim.	Testament of Simeon
T. Levi	Testament of Levi
T. Jud.	Testament of Judah
T. Iss.	Testament of Issachar
T. Zeb.	Testament of Zebulun
T. Dan	Testament of Dan
T. Naph.	Testament of Naphtali
T. Gad	Testament of Gad
T. Ash.	Testament of Asher
T. Jos.	Testament of Joseph
T. Benj.	Testament of Benjamin

DEAD SEA SCROLLS

CD	Damascus Document
1QS	Rule of the Community
4QMMT	More Works of the Torah
11QTemple	Temple Scroll
1 QSa	Rule of the Congregation
4Q398 (= 4QMMT)	Halakhic Letter

PHILO

Creation	On the Creation of the World
Drunkeness	On Drunkeness
Embassy	The Embassy to Gaius
Flaccus	Against Flaccus
Hyp	Hypothetica
Moses	The Life of Moses
Providence	On Providence
SpecLaws	On the Special Laws
Virtues	On the Virtues
QGenesis	Questions and Answers on Genesis

JOSEPHUS

Ant.	Jewish Antiquities
Apion	Against Apion
Life	Life of Josephus
War	Jewish Wars

Abbreviations

EARLY FATHERS

Pr. Ev.	Eusebius, *Praeparatio evangelica*

RABBINIC WRITINGS

A.Z.	*'Abodah Zarah*
b.	*Babylonian Talmud*
Bikk	*Bikkurim*
Gen. Rab.	*Bereshit Rabbah*
Kel.	*Kelim*
m.	*Mishnah*
Meg.	*Megillah*
Ned.	*Nedarim*
Pes.	*Pesaḥim*
Pesik. Rab.	*Pesikta Rabbati*
Sanh.	*Sanhedrin*
Shab.	*Shabbat*
t.	*Tosephta*

GREEK AND ROMAN AUTHORS

Aen.	Virgil, *Aeneid*
Ann.	Tacitus, *Annals*
Germ.	Tacitus, *The Germania*
Hist.	Tacitus, *Histories*
Hist.	Herodotus, *Histories*
Inst. Orat.	Quintilian, *Institutio Oratoria*
Sat.	Juvenal, *Satires*

MODERN SOURCES

AB	Anchor Bible
BAR	*Biblical Archaeology Review*
BDAG	Bauer, et al., editors. 2000. *A Greek-English Lexicon of the New Testament and Other Early Christian Literature.* 3rd ed. Chicago: University of Chicago Press.
BJS	Brown Judaic Studies
BTB	*Biblical Theology Bulletin*

Abbreviations

CBQ	*Catholic Biblical Quarterly*
CTW	*Criswell Theological Review*
CR: BS	*Currents in Research: Biblical Studies*
DJSS	Duke Judaic Studies Series
ERS	*Ethnic and Racial Studies*
HTR	*Harvard Theological Review*
HvTSt	*Hervormde teologiese studies*
JSHJ	*Journal for the Study of the Historical Jesus*
JSJSup	Supplements to the Journal for the Study of Judaism
JSNT	*Journal for the Study of the New Testament*
LEC	Library of Early Christianity
LTJ	*Lutheran Theological Journal*
NovT	*Novum Testamentum*
SBEC	Studies in the Bible and Early Christianity
SNTSMS	Society for New Testament Studies Monograph Series
OBT	Overtures to Biblical Theology
WUNT	Wissenschaftliche Untersuchungen zum Neuen Testament

Introduction

Sandals worn by Israelite/Judean[1] men and women consisted of leather soles and secured to the feet at the ankles with a leather strap. It was usually worn outdoors to protect the feet, while their absence meant poverty, or was a sign of respect when entering holy places. Alternatively their absence was a sign of mourning or slavery (King & Stager 2001:272–73). But when sandals were placed on the feet, the straps were tied by hands. Those hands were guided by a mind. Within that mind was a certain quality of knowledge, a certain type of mentality, a way of experiencing and looking on to the world, a way of relating to people, either seen as belonging to your own kind, or the "others." That mind was the result of social interaction, of learning, observing, touch, taste, and of conforming to values and expectations of the social group to which they belonged.

Needless to say the interior life of the average individual, especially of those separated from us by time, is inaccessible. The best we can do is to make rough approximations, assisted by the texts and archaeological evidence that they left behind. In this we can also be guided by the insights of the social sciences. After all, we are human beings ourselves subject to social processes, and if we really want to we can, to a limited extent that is, *imagine*, take a mental journey to understand the world from a differing point of view. As Christian theologians or scholars Israel is more often than not the "other," the "opponent," but what if we decide to see things also from their point of view, where Israel becomes *me*? So to walk in Israelite sandals, the metaphor employed for this study, is an attempt to investigate, understand and feel with the aggregate of minds that claimed that identity called Israel, being both the root and primary dialogue partner of our spiritual heritage.

---

1. When I refer to "Judeans," it must be understood as those Israelites living across the ancient Mediterranean who have ethnic connections to the temple-state of Judea. It replaces the anachronistic usage of "Jews."

In this book we will repeatedly refer to anthropological categories and theories, such as collectivism, honor and shame, and Israelites forming a "tight" culture, to name but a few. Yet the reader should understand that all social-scientific concepts utilized here are employed to a generalized level of abstraction. When we refer to the Israelites as forming a collectivist society, this does not mean that there were no individualists. When we speak of honor and shame, this meant different things to different people in antiquity, and also that the public code will be different from the private, especially so among subordinate groups. There will also be a difference between values propagated as an ideal and what occurs in the real world. When we speak of a "tight" culture, where people are expected to conform their actions to the social norm, this does not deny that there were subgroups (e.g., Pharisees, Essenes, etc) who formed sub-cultures, having norms and values unique to them. Neither does it mean that all people behaved according to expected norms, for if this was the case, we would not have the various Israelite/Judean sects, or the "sinners" (social deviants), least of all the existence of Christianity today. We need to follow the caution of Chance (1996:148), that when biblical scholars apply anthropological concepts they need to "(1) recognize the possibilities for heterogeneity in the societies they study, (2) develop a more sophisticated concept of culture, and (3) pay more attention to the relationship between values and practice."

Having noted the caution for variation within cultures, our study here is an attempt to have a look at the world through Israelite eyes. Again, it can be no more than an approximation, an investigation of "averages," knowing full well we are dealing with human beings, in themselves never "average," but in the very least they would have mutually shared an amount of "knowledge" and behavior because that is how they participated in a shared ethnic identity, which is the focus of our study. In the process the attempt will be made to give credence to Chance's concerns raised in numbers 2 and 3.

Why would a person be a member of the Israelite people in the first-century CE? Was it simply because they were born into that *ethnos*? Were some of the souls of the unborn (i.e., the later rabbinic concept of "Guph") destined to be born within Israel, or is Israelite birth a mere accident? But being born somewhere does not necessarily translate into staying there. Was it perhaps for economic reasons? In other words, did Israelite identity place you in a position of easy access to economic resources, or

Introduction

give you opportunities for "advancement"? Was it for political reasons, where membership in Israel gave one access to power, decision making apparatus and institutions, and distribution of above mentioned economic resources? Was it for "religious" reasons? Did the Israelites, with their monotheism and God-given law believe they were on the right "path to salvation"? Was it, perhaps, for socio-cultural reasons? In other words, being a member of Israel was about being socialized into remaining true to the customs of the fathers and inheriting an ancestry that became an indispensible part of their self-concept? Was it simply about doing what was expected, to be a welcome and competent participant of society, or was it about being somebody they believed in their hearts to be "true"?

Taking into consideration that Israelites in antiquity were an ethnic minority, and often despised at that, as well as unwilling subjects of the Roman Empire, then certainly one cannot say the reason was primarily economic or political. In Palestine they were governed by Roman prefects and procurators, or members of the Herodian dynasty, and subjected to economic exploitation. In the Diaspora they were ethnic minorities, and whatever their locale, they always had to negotiate their rights and privileges, acquiring them from Caesar or local civic authorities or with the help of influential patrons, even if they were officiating priests in the emperor cult. Certainly, being an Israelite held no economic or political privileges per se, although there were Israelites that were wealthy and through various means could obtain some political influence. Neither was it for "religious" reasons, for religion as understood today did not exist in antiquity. Religion was embedded in the social institutions of kinship and politics, and as will be assumed throughout this book, within the more comprehensive realm of Israelite ethnic identity. So why, then, be a member of an ethnic group that was so easy to identify and harass through violence or other means? Was the reason, then, perhaps to be found here, in Israel's relationship with her rich cultural tradition that embraced all aspects of life and consequently offered a meaningful and "true" view on the world?

This book does not deny the power of divine revelation, but its focus is on the more mundane processes of human culture and identity formation. Every human mind, the ancient Israelite being no different, is a blank canvass when entering the world. As that canvass is filled with the brushstrokes of experience, a picture is formed of reality, and how you relate to that reality. This study therefore testifies to my ongoing fascination with culture, especially ethnic identity, and how the insights of contemporary ethnicity theory can be applied to Biblical texts.

Already in *Jesus and Identity: Reconstructing Judean Ethnicity in Q*, I proposed a Socio-Cultural Model of Judean Ethnicity (Cromhout 2007:96–107). What this model attempted to achieve was to provide an analytical framework by which Judean or Israelite identity can be better understood. At the same time it also functions as a pictorial representation of the Judean symbolic universe, trying to explain the "world" in which Judeans lived, as well as the ethnic contents of that world. As a project it was admittedly incomplete, as some theoretical aspects of ethnicity still needed to be addressed or more coherently incorporated, the latter in particular referring to aspects of ethnicity theory which stood somewhat "isolated" from the model itself. This book serves to address these shortcomings and so must be seen as building on my earlier work.

So building on the previous venture, chapter 1 will focus on setting out a general model that will refine the theoretical approach to ethnicity. In chapter 2 these insights will be combined with the model already developed in *Jesus and Identity*, and so, it is hoped, they will together form a more comprehensive approach to Israelite ethnicity. This is also done with the recognition that research on the topic have been done and applied to the New Testament, yet small gaps in our overall approach need to be filled. I hope that the work presented in the first two chapters will help to fill these gaps.

Chapter 3 will be a conversation with the New Perspective on Paul. If you are walking in Israelite sandals, what will Paul's arguments against the "works of the law" mean to you, your identity, and sense of worth? We will investigate how Paul gave the followers of Jesus Messiah, constituting as it were a new *ethnos*, alternative core values and an alternative way of life that seriously questioned the value that attached itself to traditional Israelite identity. This provides a plausible context for why the gospel was rejected by most Israelites.

As we proceed, the invitation is given to the reader yet again to see things from a different point of view, to venture into the world of an alternative identity shaped by the social conventions of ancient Mediterranean society, that is, to walk in Israelite sandals.

1

An Introduction to Ethnicity Theory

THIS CHAPTER IS DEDICATED to the proposal and explanation of a general model of ethnicity. In the process of setting out the general model at first, it will also for the reader serve as a general introduction to ethnicity theory, bringing together some of its most important insights. Hopefully it will become obvious in the process how fruitful ethnicity theory and its application to the New Testament and/or Israelite literature can be. How fruitful this sort of interaction can be has already been demonstrated by the pioneering work of various scholars to whom I am indebted in more ways than one (e.g., Duling 2005; 2008a; 2008b; 2010; Esler 1998; 2003a; Brett 1996).

But why this preoccupation with ethnicity? It is an underlying conviction of this book that the "House of Israel" as it existed in the first century must be understood and approached as an ethnic identity, and not as a form of "religion" (cf. Stegemann 2006; Esler 2006:27). It can be argued that seeing first-century Israel as an ethnic identity—as opposed to being a form of religion—will develop to be one of the most important analytical adjustments in recent scholarship. If one reads the Bible through the lens of ethnic identity, one will proverbially see ethnic identity "screaming" for attention, and in particular illuminate our understanding of the conflict and challenges faced by the earliest followers of Jesus Messiah, as Israelites and Gentiles had to be accommodated in the same movement and which asked serious questions about identity loyalty, both old and new. The difference in emphasis argued for here may seem somewhat small if not trivial for some, yet this distinction is vital. This can be explained in an elementary form by the following contrast. For most Westerners for whom religion is in the realm of the individual and the private, being actively involved in a local church is in a way being "religious," or being a person of "faith." And being a Christian does not say anything per se about your ethnic identity. For the Israelites of the first century, however, religion was but one aspect of their overall identity. From a social-scientific perspective it is generally agreed that religion is embedded in the realms of kinship and politics, yet a modification is perhaps in order here. It can be argued that for Israelites in particular that their religion was *embedded in the more comprehensive realm of ethnicity*. This means that serving their God or living the "Judean way of life" (*Ioudaismos*)[1] was not an expression of religiosity or spirituality as such, but more an expression of their ethnic identity—it was simply being an Israelite!

It would be something akin to Brazilians playing football, African people seeking guidance from their ancestors, Afrikaners being passionate about rugby, or cowboys wearing their hats and enjoying rodeos. So for most people, whether ancient or modern, there are some things in life—which may or may not be shared by others—which lie very close to the heart. This may be the kind of sport they play, the music they make, the traditional dances they perform, the clothes they wear, the language they speak, particular food they eat, serving their god(s), or associating with a community in which these things are shared; it is part of the rich adventure of being human and making sense of the world, finding your place in the world, or simply put, having an identity! And to reiterate, for most Israelites following the "Judean way of life" it would be an expression of their ethnic identity, which would have been the equivalent of living within the covenant, obeying God's law (Torah), or to borrow from Paul, to do "works of the law."

Human beings can naturally have various social identities, some more important than others, depending on underlying value systems or social situations which require expression of an identity there and then while in other situations it may need to be suppressed. Without dismissing the importance as to the fluid nature of identity and that one can step into and out of various social roles, this book has a narrow focus, namely,

---

1. In a recent article Elliott (2007) argued that scholars must eliminate the widespread use of "Judaism" (the usual transliteration of *Ioudaismos*) altogether, as this was not a customary term of self-identification: "using 'Judaism' today as a *collective* term for Judaeans around the turn of the eras is linguistically inaccurate since it identified not a community but a type of conduct" (2007:150; emphasis original). Where the term does appear, Elliott argues we must translate it as "*Judaean way of life/behavior*" (Elliott 2007:136, 142, 150, 153). By this the usage of "Judaism" as suggested by the BDAG (2000) is also implicated as unwarranted, but I would argue that it can still be used, bearing in mind that it defines a mode of behavior, and not a social grouping as such.

in *ethnic* identity. For many peoples of the world today, it remains the primary means of self-identification. It was arguably the same for most Israelites of the first century CE, as the various writings and archaeological record of the period bear witness and to which we will often refer.

Ethnicity theory, which will drive our study here, is part of the rich and broad enterprise of social and/or cultural anthropology. It was expected at one stage that distinctive ethnicities would disappear, since their existed more and more inter-cultural contact between various ethnic groups, and the powers of globalization were also expected to diffuse such loyalties. Yet, this prediction proved to be way off the mark, since in many parts of the world ethnic affiliation still exists, and on top of that, is growing stronger, due to inter-ethnic conflict or migrant groups forming ethnic minorities. Since the 1960s in particular, ethnicity became a major topic of investigation, and part of the endeavor is to understand the underlying dynamics of ethnicity, and also to propose how ethnic conflict can be avoided and how co-existence can be accommodated (Horowitz 1985). Although ethnic affiliation can lead to all kinds of atrocities, it should not be dismissed as an inherently negative aspect of human nature, since ethnic communities can live in peaceful co-existence. According to Stanley (1996:115):

> Recent studies in comparative ethnic relations have shown that interethnic *cooperation* is more common in settings where relations between groups are highly structured; where they occupy different (and/or complementary) socioeconomic or territorial niches; where political power is distributed in a mutually acceptable (though not necessarily equal) manner; where they have equally long histories of residence in the same area; or where they share a common language and worldview and a similar set of values. Ethnic *conflict* is more likely in places where groups are competing for scarce social, economic, or territorial resources; where there are discrepancies or change in the size or political power of competing groups; where one group has migrated into the territory of another; where there is a history of conflict between groups; or where groups in the same geographical area possess discordant systems of personal and social values. (emphasis original)

Naturally, ethnic identity also provides many people with meaning—the world makes sense based on who they are, what values they hold, where they come from, the quality of life in the present, and forming a link to past and future generations.

The problem with ethnicity theory, however, is that there is still much disagreement and discussion on how ethnicity is to be defined. Is ethnicity primordial, or on the other hand constructionist, circumstantial, situational, or instrumental? More on this will be stated below, but ethnicity theory seems to be undermined by approaches that were deemed to be mutually exclusive. Some anthropologists came to see ethnicity as something difficult to wrap one's head around. It is problematic to come to grips with because it is manifested in a myriad of ways, or alternatively, plays no role whatsoever in some contexts. In effect, it is not something "out there" but only exists in observers' heads. Some have therefore argued for the deconstruction of ethnicity, where the concept is investigated in itself, but the underlying presuppositions of its representations must be critically engaged (Banks 1996). Yet a more sensible approach is to see the various approaches as mutually complimentary and that ethnicity can at any given time exhibit various characteristics with varying emphasis. This kind of integrative approach is also evident in the work of ethnicity theorists themselves (e.g., Scott 1990; Fenton 2003; Brubaker, Loveman & Stamatov 2004:49–52).

Since ethnicity theory is a modern construct, what relevance does it have on New Testament or biblical studies in general? A great deal! This must be qualified, however, by the fact that ethnicity theory uses concepts and models that would have been alien to the ancients, and they would have understood "ethnicity" on their own terms. Nevertheless, a degree of overlap is discernable. For example the word *ethnos* had a wider range of meaning in antiquity, and could refer to any grouping, human or animal, of any size. But it also acquired the meanings of "people" and "nation," referring "to a group of people with cultural, linguistic, geographical, or political unity" (Saldarini 1994:59). It also was used to refer to "other" peoples, in contrast with one's own. The plural form *ta ethnē* (also *genē*) was even more used of other peoples in contrast to one's own group, and is normally associated with ethnocentric stereotyping (Duling 2005:129; Esler 2003a:55).

There is another degree of overlap between modern ethnicity theory and ancient views of peoples, since already in antiquity people were identified by their various customs, languages, phenotypical features, ancestry, and geographical location, all features recognized today as contributing towards ethnicity. The ethnographic writings of Herodotus (*Histories*) and Tacitus (*Germania*), for example, are replete with references to traditional customs, territories, languages, rites, religious practices, ancestries, kinship and phenotypical characteristics among the people they write about.

A peculiar feature of the ancients was that they believed that the locality of various peoples engendered specific character traits "rooted in the water, soil, air, and sky native to the ethnic group" (Malina & Neyrey 1996:156), and these were passed on from parents to their offspring (Malina 1996:49). For example, look at the following stereotyping of peoples associated with specific geographical regions, as we find it in the *progymnasmata* (rhetorical handbooks):[2]

> Let us speak of what ought to be the citizens' natural character. This one might discern by looking at the famous cities of Greece and by observing how the whole inhabited world is divided up among nations. The nations inhabiting the cold places and those of Europe are full of spirit but somewhat deficient in intelligence and skill, so that they continue comparatively free, but lacking in political organization and capacity to rule their neighbors. The peoples of Asia on the other hand are intelligent and skillful in temperament, but lack spirit, so that they are in continuous subjection and slavery. But the Greek race participates in both characters, just as it occupies the middle position geographically, for it is both spirited and intelligent, hence it continues to be free and to have very good political institutions, and to be capable of ruling all mankind if it attains constitutional unity. (*Politics* 1327b.1–2)

> You will come to the topic of his native country. Here you must ask yourself whether it is a distinguished country or not [and whether he comes from a celebrated and splendid place or not]. If his country is famous, you should place your account of it first, and mention it before his family ... If the city has no distinction, you must inquire whether his nation as a whole is considered brave and valiant, or is devoted to literature or the possession of virtues, like the Greek race, or again is distinguished for law, like the Italian, or is courageous, like the Gauls or Paeonians. You must argue that it is inevitable that a man from such a [city or] or nation should have such characteristics. (*Menander Rhetor* 2.369.18—370.5)

---

2. See also Quintilian, *Inst. Orat.* 3.7.10–18. I would like to thank Jerome Neyrey for supplying me with these texts. See also the discussion of Esler (2003a:59–60) on Hippocrates' *Airs, Waters, Places*.

Ethnic groups were therefore subject to stereotyping, and unlike modern sensitivities, having certain characteristics were seen as a "natural" part of life. People were not so much self-made or socialized into a way of life, they were understood to be born with it. It was something flowing through their veins. For Israelites the phenomenon of stereotyping of the "other" also applies, but perhaps for other reasons. They would have understood themselves as "kingdom of priests and a holy people (*ethnos hagion*)" (Exod 19:6), in contrast to Gentiles who are "impure" or morally degenerate, because they were not elected by God and did not receive his Law. However it came to be, stereotyping was part and parcel of the ancient way of identifying your own or other "peoples" and gives further evidence that what we understand today as "ethnic groups" had their equivalent in antiquity.

It can also be argued that ethnic groups existed in the biblical world, if not at all periods, ever since humankind decided to group together in more or less permanent settlements (cf. Duling 2005:127–29; Esler 2003a:53). According to Anthony Smith (1986:32–46; 1997) ethnic communities played an active part in human society from at least the third millennium BCE. He suggests that what helped to shape ethnic groups were (1) *sedentarization and nostalgia*, where pastoral and nomadic lifestyles were replaced with small village settlements. This led to the creation of local folk culture and ties, to which was attached a nostalgia for the past; (2) *organized religion*, where ethnic origins were explained through mythical tales and connected with religious beliefs about creation. Religion also helped to communicate ethnic myths and symbols; and (3) *inter-state warfare* between different kinds of political authority. Smith (1986:46) concludes that "ethnicity provides one of the central axes of alignment and division in the pre-modern world, and one of the most durable."

For now let us focus our attention on the general model of ethnicity that will be proposed here. It is not claimed that it is original in its insights, but what it attempts to do is to bring together some of the most important aspects of ethnicity theory, aspects which can prove to be most helpful when we investigate Israelite ethnic identity in further detail. It is also a work in progress, an experiment, always subject to critique, improvement or correction; in a word, it is heuristic. It is there to serve as a guide, not as analytical dogma, being an aid in terms of what questions can be asked in biblical studies and what social and cultural processes are to be expected.

An Introduction to Ethnicity Theory

I am indebted to Jenkins (1997:165)[3] and his model which provides the inspiration and bulk of the approach taken here but is at the same time "fleshed out" with other insights as well in the attempt to make it more user friendly and understandable. The proposed model looks as follows:

A General Model of Ethnicity

1. *Ethnicity is a form of social identity and relation*, referring to a group of people who ascribe to themselves and/or by others, a sense of belonging and a shared cultural tradition;

2. *Ethnicity is socially (re)constructed*, the outcome of enculturation and socialization, as well as the social interaction with "others" across the ethnic boundary;

3. *Ethnicity is about cultural differentiation*, involving the communication of similarity vis-à-vis co-ethnics (aggregative "we") and the communication of difference in opposition to ethnic others (oppositional "we-they");

4. *Ethnicity is concerned with culture—shared meaning—*which consists of any combination of the following: widely accepted values/norms which govern behavior, a corporate name for the group, myths of common ancestry, shared "historical" memories, an actual or symbolic attachment to a specific territory or ancestral land, a shared language or dialect, kinship patterns, shared customs, a shared religion, and shared phenotypical or genetic features;

5. *Ethnicity is no more fixed than the culture of which it is a component*, or the situations in which it is produced and reproduced;

6. *Ethnicity is both collective and individual*, externalized in social interaction and internalized in personal self-identification.

---

3. Jenkins has proposed a "basic social anthropological model" of ethnicity, which he presents as a set of loosely linked propositions, which is as follows:
- Ethnicity is about cultural differentiation (bearing in mind that identity is always a dialectic between similarity and difference);
- Ethnicity is concerned with culture—shared meaning—but it is also rooted in, and the outcome of, social interaction;
- Ethnicity is no more fixed than the culture of which it is a component, or the situations in which it is produced and reproduced;
- Ethnicity is both collective and individual, externalized in social interaction and internalized in personal self-identification.

It should be noted that the last two propositions of Jenkins's model are left intact. But now we will proceed to clarify the model by giving each statement an explanation. Israelite and other ancient authors and texts will also be employed to give the explanations further intelligibility, while at the same time, it will test, and hopefully demonstrate the model for its overall usability.

1. *Ethnicity is a form of social identity and relation*, referring to a group of people who ascribe to themselves and/or by others, a sense of belonging and a shared cultural tradition.

Ethnicity is one form of social identity among many. It refers to a group of people that have a special—mostly cultural—*relation* to each other. They share a feeling of mutual belongingness, or they have a sense of solidarity. Depending on the circumstances, ethnic identification may be important, while in others it may be secondary or even irrelevant. But especially in collectivist societies (cf. Malina 1993), ethnic identity is salient, more so than in individualistic societies. Theissen (1992:216–19, 274–76) refers to the strong sense of solidarity among the "Jews," or rather, Judeans/Israelites in antiquity, which extended across political boundaries, which was enhanced by what he calls "supraregional communication." This solidarity was also recognized by outsiders (e.g., Tacitus *Hist.* 5.5.1). The latter increased the Greek suspicion of the Israelites, as their solidarity helped to preserve their identity, and helped to avoid their assimilation into Greek culture.

Belonging to an ethnic group is like belonging to a form of extended kinship. Horowitz (1985:81) draws attention to the needs served by ethnicity, which is similar to that of kinship: familiarity and community, family-like ties to counter isolation in complex societies, emotional support and reciprocal help, and mediation and dispute resolution. As opposed to kinship, ethnicity meets these needs on a larger canvas. This idea of ethnicity being an extended form of kinship is evident in Cicero:

> Now there are several levels in human society. Apart from mankind as a whole ... there is the more restricted level of belonging to the same race, the same tribe, and the same language: these join men together very closely. An even closer relationship is to belong to the same city ... Even closer are the ties among a group of relatives ... When a single house cannot shelter all of them, they migrate to other houses as if they were going out to colonies. Marriages and alliances of families deriving from these marriages follow, and they

> result in even more relatives. These propagations and offshoots are the beginning of states. So blood relationship links men together in good will and affection; for it is worth a great deal to have common ancestral monuments, to employ the same religious rites, and to possess common burial places. (*On Duties* 1.53–54)

Here Cicero connects the positive elements of extended kinship ("blood relationship") with having a common cultural tradition.

Group membership and identity have been evaluated along three "dimensions," namely, the "cognitive," "evaluative," and "emotional." These relate to the sense of belonging that is shared among social groups. These were brought to our attention by Esler (1996:226–27), who himself drew on the work of Henri Tajfel (1978; 1981), and are generally known as social identity theory, where he investigated group membership and inter-group dynamics. It works as follows. The "cognitive" dimension is the recognition of belonging to a group; the "evaluative" dimension relates to positive or negative connotations of belonging to a group; the "emotional" has to do with attitudes towards insiders and outsiders. These three dimensions are closely interrelated and feed off each other as will be set out below.

The cognitive dimension has to do with the ubiquitous phenomenon of categorization. Categories are mental constructs, where the world is simplified and ordered in specific ways. It is also reductionist, as it follows the principle of "cognitive economy," where the most amount of information is accessed with the least effort. This applies to the way you see, interpret and do things, to avoid being overcome by all the stimuli around you, and so the world becomes more manageable. Categorizations create "knowledge" and expectations, and things become "predictable" as people, events, and objects are mostly subconsciously placed within categories. This insight extends to social identity theory, or the later development of self-categorization theory, where we encounter the process of *social categorization*, that is, where people classify themselves and others into groups. Turner (1987) and his approach known as self-categorization theory observed that social categorization is a fundamental aspect of group behavior. Here mental or cognitive processes are also reductionist, as differences between people are minimized, whether they belong to your "in-group" or "out-group." So what we find is an exaggeration of similarities between people of the same group, as well as the exaggeration of differences between people of different categories.

Tajfel's (1981) study of interaction between groups suggested that members tend to favor the in-group. Both Tajfel and Turner also argued that the mere recognition of belonging to two different groups triggers intergroup discrimination. Thus in-group bias goes hand in hand with intergroup comparison, which involve negative stereotyping of the out-group and positive stereotyping of the in-group. These negative features of intergroup relations are seen to manifest themselves because merely through the recognition of belonging that you belong to a group, people categorize themselves in view of the need to distinguish themselves and to create a positive self-value vis-à-vis other groups (Tajfel & Turner 1979). These features, however, need not always occur, and subsequent studies have shown that they are more distinctive of collectivist and competitive groups (Brown 1995; 2001). Both these features characterize all ancient Mediterranean peoples. So the Israelites were typically collectivists[4] or group-orientated persons. They were "embedded" in groups such as the family, *ethnos*, fictive families, the synagogue, patron-client networks, and the *polis* or village (cf. Malina & Neyrey 2008:260–63).

As opposed to western individualism, collectivists (which also characterizes about 70% of the world's population today) regard the group you belong to as the primary point of reference and more important than the concerns, preferences, or self-expression of the individual. You always act as a representative of the group and you must embody its values. The group is your primary focus of loyalty. The group sets the standard for acceptable behavior and appropriate action. It is from the group that you derive your sense of identity. Instead of it being a matter of "me," "myself" and "I," it is about "us," "we" and "our." "*Our* Father in heaven . . . ," Jesus taught his disciples. The Israelites also found themselves in an agonistic (competitive) social context because of the rivalry for honor. Due to the notion of "limited good" persons or groups could only gain honor at the expense of others, something continually contested in the social game of

---

4. I say "typically," because as Triandis points out, collectivism and individualism are central tendencies. One must also deal with variability within cultures. Within both collectivist and individualistic societies there are individuals who are countercultural. "There are idiocentrics in collectivist cultures and allocentrics in individualistic cultures . . ." (Triandis 1994a:289). The individualism-collectivism contrast as two polar opposites has also been criticized for its generality, as the kind of collectivism in any society may be different in quality depending on who the target group is (e.g., peers, wife, family, society etc) (Berry, Poortinga, Segall & Dasen 2002:65–71). This latter insight is certainly relevant to groups such as the Pharisees and Essenes.

challenge and riposte.[5] So ancient Israelites would have been in an environment favorable to produce in-group bias and intergroup comparison (cf. Esler 1998:46–48).

Ethnicity as a form of cognition in itself has only very recently been addressed, although as an analytic method it was laying beneath the surface. So Banks (1996) is correct in that ethnicity is something in people's heads; it is not something restricted to observers, but exists in *everybody's* head, whether you are observing or participating. Ethnicity has been described as the interface between the mind, society, and culture, or between the individual and the body of knowledge that exists beyond him or her (cf. Levine 1999; Mahmood & Armstrong 1992). Ethnic identities "are not things *in* the world, but perspectives *on* the world—not ontological but epistemological realities" (Brubaker, Loveman & Stamatov 2004:45; emphasis original). It is the way that people categorize themselves and others, create identities, similarities and differences, and organize social knowledge and legitimate their actions.

To reiterate, groups are a source of identity. By belonging to a group people derive a sense of who they are as well as a sense of worth (Brown 2001). So the "evaluative" dimension, now appreciating it especially within the agonistic Mediterranean context, has to do with that perpetual human delusion that whatever group you belong to (ethnic or otherwise) is "the best." Look at what Herodotus had to say about this already two and a half millennia ago:

> For if anyone, no matter who, were given the opportunity of choosing from amongst all the nations in the world the beliefs which he thought best, he would inevitably, after careful consideration of their relative merits, choose those of his own country. Everyone without exception believes his own native customs, and the religion he was brought up in, to be the best; and that being so, it is unlikely that anyone but a madman would mock at such things. There is abundant evidence that this is the universal feeling about the ancient customs of one's country. (*Hist.* 3.37)

---

5. Societies where social competition for perceived limited resources are encountered are referred to as "agonistic societies." The notion of "limited good" has to do with a view of the world where resources (e.g., honor, wealth) are in finite supply. It was therefore traditionally expected for persons to maintain their social status, not to enhance it. If somehow their status was enhanced, that status they must have taken from somebody else. A person/group's gain was seen as another person/group's loss (Neyrey & Rohrbaugh 2008).

So part and parcel of attachment to an ethnic group is that group members desire a positive valuation of their own group and which can be compared favorably with others (Esler 1996; 1998:42–48; Horowitz 1985:143–47). In a similar fashion, the Israelites were socialized into a symbolic universe filled with positive identity characteristics, which was believed to set them apart from other peoples and groups. In addition to collective honor, their identity encoded attributes such as righteousness, a distinguished ancestry, morality, divine favor, and monotheism. They had the understanding of being God's elected people, chosen from among all the nations to be his special possession. This meant they were set apart for God, which required a degree of separation from the Gentiles. What distinguished them was their worship of the true Creator; they did not participate in the folly of idolatry like the Gentiles. God also made a covenant with them, which entailed the privilege of having received his Law. This Law described holy conduct and how to distinguish between what is pure/clean and impure/unclean. It is of eternal value (Sir 24:9; 33; 1 Bar 4:1; WisSol 18:4; *T. Naph.* 3:1–2). It was also the basis on which the Israelites claimed moral superiority, and this kind of social differentiation or comparison normally exacerbates the denigration and contempt for outgroups (Brewer 1999:435).[6] Gentiles were generally stereotyped as "sinners" (e.g., *Jub*. 23:24).

The following texts can be used to illustrate this further. The Gentiles were often criticized for idolatry and sexual immorality. It is said to the Gentiles: "You neither revere nor fear God, but wander to no purpose, worshipping snakes and sacrificing to cats, speechless idols, and stone statues of people; and sitting in front of the doors at godless temples you do not fear the existing God who guards all things" (*Sib. Or.* 3:30–34).[7] The Greeks are "overbearing and impious" (*Sib. Or.* 3:171). There is the

---

6. Brewer (1999:435–38) lists moral superiority, along with the perceived threat of outgroups, the sharing of common goals, the sharing of common values which result in competitive social comparison, as well as power politics as some of the ways in which "the conditions of maintaining ingroup integrity and loyalty pave the way to outgroup hate and hostility."

7. Idolatry is also attacked in *Sib. Or.* 3:545–54; 5:276–80; 5:484–500; *T. Job* 2:2—3:3, 5:2; *T. Mos* 2:8–9; *Let. Aris.* 134–35; *Jub.* 12:2–5; 20:7–9; 21:5; 22:18, 22. It is also said that Judeans do not commit adultery and "do not engage in impious intercourse with male children, as do Phoenicians, Egyptians, and Romans, spacious Greece and many nations of others, Persians and Galatians and all Asia, transgressing the holy law of immortal God" (*Sib. Or.* 3:596–600; cf. *Sib. Or.* 4:33–34; 5:430).

warning not to "become involved in revolting gentile affairs" (*T. Jud.* 23:2; cf. *T. Dan.* 5:5, 8). The Gentiles are "abominable and lawless" (*3 Macc* 6:9, 12). The deeds of Gentiles are "defilement and corruption and contamination; and there is no righteousness with them" (*Jub.* 21:21). In contrast, the Judeans are "a race of most righteous" or "pious men" (*Sib. Or.* 3:219; 3:573).

Israelites also compared themselves favorably with other peoples in other ways. Gruen (2002) has demonstrated how the literature of this period (the Apocrypha and Pseudepigrapha in particular) was used to emphasize the superiority of the Israelite heritage, and how it functioned to boost Israelite self-esteem, or we can say, their honor ranking. The figures of Joseph, Enoch, Abraham, and Moses were variously used to stress Israelite advantage and superiority vis-à-vis the Gentiles. These figures were presented as the founders of astrology, science, as the originators of human knowledge, culture, the alphabet, and Greek poetry and philosophy. Israelite heroes are represented as shrewd, clever, and resourceful, who easily mock, manipulate, and outwit their Gentile overlords. They do all this while still obtaining their favor, both for themselves and the Israelite people. Other authors wrote of how the Hellenistic kings stood in awe of the Israelite faith, wisdom, and culture. Various rulers also depended on Israelite wit and faith for their achievements and successes. Gruen's analysis is therefore helpful to us in terms of how the Israelite authors employed positive stereotyping of their "in-group" and how they presented Israelites as comparing favourably with "out-groups." Claims of Israelite superiority in character, values, intelligence, and beliefs were underlined by these authors for their people living in a world not of their own making, and which made political subordination palatable.

As for the "emotional" dimension, it can be mentioned that social behavior in collectivist societies, of which Israel was an example, tend to be dependent, emotionally attached, and involved in the collective. It is also cooperative and self-sacrificing towards in-group members, but indifferent and even hostile to out-group members (Triandis 1994a:287). According to Cicero, "when we choose among moral duties, the group that takes precedence is the one based on the idea of social harmony ... first duties are owed to the immortal gods, second duties to the fatherland, third ones to the parents..." (*On Duties* 1.160). Josephus states: "Our sacrifices are not occasions for drunken self-indulgence—such practices are abhorrent to God—but for sobriety. At these sacrifices prayers for the welfare of the community must take precedence of those for ourselves; for we are born for fellowship, and he who sets its claims above his private interests is specially acceptable to God" (*Apion* 2.195–96). The in-group collective is the primary concern—in the very least, that was the ideal.

Out-groups on the other hand, are fair game, objects of suspicion and hostility. The various Israelite texts already cited above clearly demonstrate this. We can also think of the Israelite refusal to eat with Gentiles (*Jub.* 22:16; *Let. Aris.* 139–42; Gal 2:12); or to buy their produce, such as bread, wine, cheese, and oil; or to intermarry. On pain of death, Gentiles were forbidden to enter the temple's inner courts (Josephus *Ant.* 15.417; Philo *Embassy* 212; cf. Acts 21:27–31). Juvenal says Judeans will show the way only to fellow Judeans, and will direct only the circumcised to a well (*Sat.* 14.103–4). Whether true or not, it testifies to in-group versus out-group dynamics that a person can tend to expect in the first-century social context. After all, some Samaritans according to Josephus (*Ant.* 18.30) scattered human bones (considered ritually impure) in the temple in Jerusalem during the tenure of Coponius (6–9 CE), and so demonstrated complete indifference towards Israelite sensibilities.

Not much will be said here about ethnicity comprising a shared cultural tradition, as this is further explored in the pages that follow. For now it points the obvious conclusion that people who have a sense of belonging also have much in common, such as a shared culture for ethnic groups. (For more information on this see the explanation of point 4 of the model.)

2. *Ethnicity is socially (re)constructed*, the outcome of enculturation and socialization, as well as the social interaction with "others" across the ethnic boundary.

The dominant perspective in ethnicity theory today is that ethnicity is *socially (re)constructed* (known as constructionism or constructivism). This builds on the work of Frederik Barth (1969; cf. Barth 1994:12). Barth initially argued that the "cultural stuff," although important for social boundaries, is "not as important as the act *of social boundary marking itself*" (Duling 2005:127; emphasis original). Constructionists took this further, and in reaction to primordialism (see elaboration of point 5 below) argued that "ethnic identity is not inherent, fixed, or natural; rather, it is *fluid, freely chosen*, and thus can be seen to be *perpetually constructed, that is, continually reconstructed*" (Duling 2005:127; emphasis original). Downplaying the importance of the "cultural stuff" of ethnic groups, the emphasis came to be on *how* and *why* ethnic groups create and maintain their group boundaries. Here the boundary between an ethnic group and outsiders is perceived more as a process than a barrier, thus "cultural features of the ethnic group are the visible and variable manifestation, but not the cause, of an ethnic boundary and identity . . . [C]ultural indicia might change over time and yet the ethnic group could still retain a sense of its own distinctiveness" (Esler 2003a:42–43). Cultural features do not constitute, but *signal* ethnic identity and boundaries. An ethnic identity is maintained but with *no necessary relation to specific cultural content*—the ethnic identity is self-ascriptive, continuously renewed and renegotiated through social practice (Esler 2003a:42, 47). As will be discussed below, taken at face value constructionists give a somewhat narrow view of ethnicity. There is far more to ethnic identity than the mere preoccupation to maintain a group's social boundaries.

A major development based on constructionism is instrumentalism, where an ethnic group's self-construction is rational and self-interested and consciously mobilized in an attempt to further its own political-economic agenda (Duling 2005:127; Esler 2003a:46). In this scenario an ethnic group can also be identified as an *interest group* (Bernstein 1984:100). Similar approaches are variously known as "circumstantial" and "situational." The "circumstantial" approach sees ethnic identity as important in some contexts but not in others. The identity remains constant but whether it matters is determined by circumstances. The "situational" perspective claims that identity is expressed in different ways as the social situations of the individual change. This is relevant where a social actor possesses more than one ethnic identity (Esler 2003a:49)—in fact, most, if not all social actors do. It can be due to having parents of differing ethnic groups, or this "situational" identity is derived from identifying yourself with people of a local and smaller regional area, or alternatively, this identity can fade into the background when a situation requires identification with a larger or national grouping. For example, when people from Judea and Galilee engage in social interaction, they will respectively activate their Judean and Galilean identities. When both of these interact with Gentiles, however, they will activate the more encompassing Israelite or Judean (in its broader sense) identity. What sets all these approaches apart from primordialism is the element of *choice* in how or what ethnic identity is manifested on the part of the social agents in question. Sometimes some of these terms are used interchangeably, since "instrumental" and "situational" models are treated as part of the "circumstantial" approach (Scott 1990:148), or "instrumentalism" it is said is sometimes known as the "circumstantialist" approach (Banks 1996:39).

Now attention will be drawn to two ways through which ethnicity is socially (re)constructed. Firstly, it is not just about the construction of social boundaries. This view can be seen as making human beings somewhat soulless creatures. For some or other reason, not sufficiently explained, they need to distinguish between "us" and "them." Yet, the matter runs deeper, referring to underlying psychological reasons why ethnic (dis)association exists. That is why the model explains first that ethnicity is the outcome of enculturation and socialization. The approach here favors the argument that ethnicity is logically and ontologically prior to any boundary between "us" and "them" (Roosens 1994:85–87), but it also appreciates that the relationship should be seen as dialectic. Social and cross-cultural psychology explains: "Enculturation takes place by the 'enfolding' of individuals by their culture, leading them to incorporate appropriate behaviour into their repertoires. Socialization takes place by more specific instruction and training, again leading to the acquisition of culture-appropriate behaviour" (Berry, Poortinga, Segall & Dasen 2002:21).

In enculturation, deriving from cultural anthropology, there is no specific training or teaching as such, but the individual learns how to become competent in his/her culture—its language, rituals, values and so on—through a network of various influences (parents, other adults, peers). The process of enculturation is similar to a concept known as the "habitus," a theoretical term drawn from Bourdieu's (1977) theory of practice. The *habitus* consists of durable dispositions, or "unreflexive habit" (Jenkins 1994:203; 1997:58; 2003:64), that produce certain perceptions and practices.[8] These perceptions and practices "become part of an individual's sense of self at an early age, and which can be transposed from one context to another ... As such, the *habitus* involves a process of socialization whereby new experiences are structured in accordance with the structures produced by past experiences, and early experiences re-

---

8. This can be connected to the sociological study of "schemata," culturally shared mental constructs, which both represent and process information. "They guide perception and recall, interpret experience, generate inferences and expectations, and organize action" (Brubaker et al. 2004:41; and see 42). A feature of schemata (also known as scripts, maps, frames, models) is that they are inherently resistant to change.

tain a particular weight" (Jones 1997:88). So the *habitus* function as both "structuring structures" and "structured structures," which shape, and are shaped by social practice (Jones 1997:89). This approach can also be applied to the realm of ethnicity. Bentley used Bourdieu's theory of practice to develop a *practice theory of ethnicity*: "According to the practice theory of ethnicity, sensations of ethnic affinity are founded on common life experiences that generate similar habitual dispositions ... It is commonality of experience and of the preconscious habitus it generates that gives members of an ethnic cohort their sense of being both familiar and familial to each other" (Bentley 1987:32–33).

Bentley developed this theory in response to constructionists who took the Barthian view to an extreme, where ethnic attachment was exclusively seen as the result of social differentiation, yet he does not deny its abiding importance (Bentley 1991). It was a matter of getting the balance right, focusing also on processes within a group (the similarities) as much as those that exist between groups (the differences). So it can be argued that the "intersubjective construction of ethnic identity is grounded in the shared subliminal dispositions of the *habitus* which shape, and are shaped by, objective commonalities of practice ... The cultural practices and representations that become objectified as symbols of ethnicity are derived from, and resonate with, the habitual practices and experiences of the people involved, as well as reflecting the instrumental contingencies and meaningful cultural idioms of a particular situation" (Jones 1997:90).

The *habitus* can be extended to incorporate the process of socialization, which developed in the disciplines of sociology and social psychology and that refers to deliberate shaping of the individual. It refers to social actors receiving specific instruction. Important for our purposes, however, is that the "eventual result of both enculturation and socialization is the development of behavioral similarities within cultures, and behavioral differences between cultures. They are thus the crucial cultural mechanisms that produce the distribution of similarities and differences" (Berry et al. 2002:30). And cultural transmission from one generation to the next usually falls close to the full transmission end of the scale (as opposed to the non-transmission end).

From the above it can be gathered that one of the results of enculturation and socialization also has to do with the human search for meaning (see also point 4 below). Who are we? Why do we do the things we do? Where is my place in society? What does God or the ancestors expect?

Where do we come from? More about this search for meaning will be said in chapter 2 where we will focus on Israel's "symbolic universe," as it relates to their world of meaning being brought together into an integrated whole. For now we can mention that people are surrounded by what has been described as the "plausibility system" (Berger 1967; Bell 1997:256–57). It refers to the network of people around you and who share your beliefs, giving them the appearance of being the right understanding of the true nature of things. The local community or peer groups are important role players in this regard, but the family is the most important conduit of the plausibility system.

For the Israelites of the first century, the above-mentioned dynamics also apply. Be it through observing, participating, or receiving specific instruction that both formed and derived from a social and mental space of "habitual dispositions" (*habitus*), it contributed to them having a particular way of looking at the world. Everyday life for Israelites was regulated by their divine patron, Yahweh, the requirements of the Torah, and of course, the general values and norms of society. For example, they lived in a symbolic universe that had a set rhythm, a "map of time" (cf. Neyrey 1990), structured by the weekly cycle of the Sabbath, the annual cycle of the feasts, and when you could work. They were exposed to regulations of what and how you could eat, how you must prepare your food, and other dietary or purity regulations as well (cf. Stegemann & Stegemann 1999:142). They grew up in symbolic universe that set out a "map of persons," distinguishing those whom properly belonged from the "other," and where social interaction was permitted or should be avoided, and so more features of their "world" can be listed.

Specific instruction could be mediated through the local assembly (synagogue), but was also the particular responsibility of the father towards his son. The Tanak in various passages (Exod 12:26–27; 13:14–15; Deut 6:20–24; Josh 4:6–7, 21–23) specifies that the father must explain an event, memory, or institution. So the exodus, the conquest and the gift of the land, and their common history would be explained (Tobit 4; 4 Macc 18:10–19; Philo, *SpecLaws* 4.150; Josephus *Apion* 1.60; *m. Pes.* 10:4). According to Josephus Judeans are commanded: "to bring [Judean] children up in learning and to exercise them in the laws, and make them acquainted with the acts of their predecessors, in order to their imitation of them, and that they might be nourished up in the laws from their infancy, and might neither transgress them, nor have any pretence for their ignorance of them" (*Apion* 2.204).

In addition to this we may think of the Essenes, Pharisees, and the *haberim* or associates, which had their own specialized forms or authorities of instruction. But for the average Israelite the process of enculturation and socialization had as its aim for individuals to embody the traditions and to emulate the example of the ancestors. Ethnicity is a social identity where commitment is primarily, but not exclusively, orientated to the past (cf. De Vos 1975:17–19; Malina & Neyrey 1996:166; Guijarro 2001:227).

Secondly, ethnic (re)construction is also the outcome of social interaction with "others" across the ethnic boundary. Here the boundary between an ethnic group and others are negotiated or (re)constructed, using various symbols and cultural practices. This is usually a combination of the new and the old, but at any given moment either the more traditional or the invention of new emblems of identity can be given the greater emphasis, depending on the nature of the social and historical context.

For example, when we look at the circumstances of the Maccabean crisis Israelites had to protect the integrity of their identity against the onslaughts of Hellenism (1 Macc 1:11–13). During this period covenantal praxis—such as circumcision, food laws, and Sabbath observance—were targeted by Antiochus IV Epiphanes for extinction. Why? Because these practices, amongst others, were in conflict with his policy of integrating the various peoples in the Seleucid Empire. How did the Israelites respond? Of course, they revolted under the leadership of the Maccabees; but more significant for our purposes is that ever since this period these covenantal praxis gained prominence in Israelite identity and self-understanding (Dunn 1990:193). They had to engage in a heightened form of boundary maintenance or (re)construction to remain distinct from the universal and all-embracing culture of Hellenism. It is said that Moses "surrounded us with unbroken palisades and iron walls to prevent our mixing with any of the other peoples in any matter, being thus kept pure in body and soul, preserved from false beliefs, and worshipping the only God omnipotent over all creation . . . So, to prevent our being perverted by contact with others or mixing with bad influences, he hedged us in on all sides with strict observances connected with meat and drink and touch and hearing and sight, after the manner of the Law" (*Let. Aris.* 139–42).

Peter was reproached by the "circumcision party" after his return from Caesarea: "You went into the house of uncircumcised men and ate with them" (Acts 11:3). Peter was again accused, but this time by Paul for hypocrisy because of his withdrawal from table fellowship with the Gentiles in Antioch (Gal 2:12–13). This all relates to how the boundary of the social group needed to be negotiated according to the expected norm, and Peter found himself being tugged between two opposing views. For most Israelites, he would not only have undermined their social boundary, but also betrayed the heroes of the Maccabean revolt and the popular figures of Daniel, Tobit, Judith, Esther, and Joseph, who all showed their faithfulness to God: that is, they maintained their Israelite identity by refusing to eat "the food of Gentiles" (Dan 1:8–16; 10:3; Tob 1:10–13; Jdt 10:5; 12:1–20; AddEsth 14:17; *Jos. Asen.* 7:1; 8:5). These texts, rich in ethno-symbolism,[9] depict people as heroes because they were faithful Israelites, examples to emulate.[10] They negotiated their ethnic boundary in the correct way.

So as a result of the Maccabean crisis, Israelite ethnicity was in part (re)constructed around an intensified effort to observe food and purity laws more strictly, which along with a concern for circumcision, Sabbath observance, and the temple in Jerusalem, characterized the Israelite attitude throughout this period.

Another example of this (re)constructionist tendency occurs after the Roman annexation of Palestine. One of the Maccabean aims was to expand Israelite territory, which they saw as nothing other than their

---

9. Ethno-symbolism analyses how an ethnic group's nostalgia about its perceived past—expressed through cosmogonic myths, election myths, memories of a golden age, symbols—shapes the group's ability to endure, but also to change and adapt (Duling, 2005:127). This can also be seen in other Judean literature (e.g., *Jubilees* and *L.A.B.*) where past traditions are used creatively for the Judean struggle against Hellenism.

10. Aguilar (2000) speaks of historical narratives or the perception and interpretation of the past as "ethnographic realities," concerned about continuity and the future, more so than the past itself. Ethnographic materials become an "archaeology of memory, buried in the past, however relevant for the present and for the future of any given society" (2000:65). Commenting on the production of Maccabean literature: "The production of this sort of narrative is important for successive generations of Jews because it shows that a small nation can stand against a mighty power if and only if such a nation has a common bond of ethnicity and identity related to a common myth of origin. Such a myth needs to be actualized and reinvented throughout history by the creation of heroes that decide to maintain their distinct identity against all pressures for cultural accommodation and syncretistic acculturation" (Aguilar 2000:62).

rightful possession, the "inheritance of our fathers" (1 Macc 15:33). With this they either forced the Gentiles to convert within the conquered territories, or forced them to leave. When Palestine became part of the Roman Empire this spatial separation between Israelite and Gentile was no longer possible. How can one maintain the identity and boundary of the House of Israel in this case? Apart from the usual practises, here enters the prominence of ritual immersion. Since the separation could no longer be spatial, it became ritual, clearly delineating those who participate in Israelite identity from those who do not (Stegemann & Stegemann 1999:143; Schmidt 2001:239). Immersion pools (*miqva'ot,* singular *mikveh)* dating to this period have been found all over Judea, Galilee, and the Golan. Apart from contact with Gentiles or others of "impure" status, ritual immersion also removed impurity after sexual intercourse, menstruation, child birth, contact with a human corpse, and was also necessary to gain access to the temple. And so the perfect order of God's creation (and indeed, Israelite identity) thus encoded on the margins and integrity of Israelite bodies, could be maintained. And as the study of Mary Douglas (1966) informs us, the physical body is a symbolic representation or microcosm of the larger society. Preservation of the integrity of the physical body—in this instance through ritual immersion—preserves the identity, integrity, and social boundary of Israel as a whole.

3. *Ethnicity is about cultural differentiation*, involving the communication of similarity vis-à-vis co-ethnics (aggregative "we") and the communication of difference in opposition to ethnic others (oppositional "we-they").

Ethnicity is about cultural differentiation. It involves the communication of similarity and difference. "Communicating" does not refer here to verbal aspects, but more so to *doing* something. You communicate that you belong to a particular ethnic group, while at the same time you communicate cultural differentiation from the "other." In this manner you embody in your own person and behavior the boundary (re)construction process already discussed above. Constructionists also explain that groups construct their ethnic boundaries in two major ways: firstly "in relation to like-minded, like-practiced peers, a 'we' *aggregative* self-definition" and secondly, "in relation to *others*, a 'we-they' *oppositional* self-definition." The latter is usually ethnocentric (Duling 2005:127).

The kind of doing (= communicating) spoken of here, that is, when appreciated within the context of collectivist societies, puts emphasis on *orthopraxy*, rather than orthodoxy. This does not mean that there is no required standard of "orthodoxy" or set of values that beg allegiance, but while still important, it plays a secondary role. It is a matter of emphasis. In (Western) Christian tradition, emphasis is placed on correct beliefs, adhering to what is seen as correct creedal formulas or statements of faith: "I believe in God the Father . . . ," etc. In traditional collectivist societies the emphasis is different. Where social, religious, political, and cultural aspects are closely intertwined for a group, how you participate in a community's customs, rituals and obligations are far more important than adhering to a set of beliefs. If you perform the proper rituals, dress in the right way, participate in festivals, or eat the right kind of foods, these are the vital elements which illustrate you are an integral part of the community. Extreme forms of orthopraxy are "the very means by which a group heightens and maintains its internal group identity, often in the face of more diffused and complacent communities" (Bell 1997:193).

When Israelites observed covenantal praxis, their "ancestral customs," they communicated their identity, that is, their belonging and similarity vis-à-vis co-ethnics and difference or "distinctiveness" in opposition to ethnic outsiders. That is why Israel was also defined more by orthopraxy than by orthodoxy (Cohen 1987:61, 103; Schmidt 2001:25). In other words, *doing* (= *communicating*) was given greater prominence than having the right "theology" or "faith." Sadducees did not believe in the resurrection, but in the first century they were not "excommunicated" from Israelite society (Acts 23:8). We can therefore equate orthopraxy with the act of "communication." To perform covenantal praxis or "works of the law" was to communicate their (privileged) Israelite ethnic identity, that they belong to and participated in God's covenant blessings and salvation as it applied to a select group of people. This was to follow the "Judean way of life" (*Ioudaismos*) bearing witness to an identity that encoded divine favor. The importance of orthopraxy, and therefore the act of "communication" as well, becomes evident in the comments of Josephus who defines an apostate as a Judean who "hates the customs of the Judeans" or "does not abide by the ancestral customs" (*War* 7.50; *Ant.* 20.100). He describes a convert as a Gentile who through circumcision "adopts the ancestral customs of the Judeans" (*Ant.* 20.17, 41), a sentiment also held by Philo (*Virtues* 102–8). And when one thinks of the various sects in the "Judean way of life," these were not various ways of being "religious." They were different ways of communicating Israelite ethnic identity.

An Introduction to Ethnicity Theory

The House of Israel can also be understood as a "tight culture," where norms and values had to be followed more strictly. It can be associated with collectivist cultures where people are criticized for minor deviations from what is seen as proper behavior, and where there are normally very strong feelings about the integrity of their in-group. Social behavior is therefore a function of norms and duties imposed by the collective, and as already mentioned, tends to be dependent, emotionally attached, and involved in the collective. Behavior is expected to be cooperative and self-sacrificing, where the requirements of the group are placed above individual needs (cf. Triandis 1994a:287; 1994b:159–72). And in collectivist societies it is typical to control behavior through the emotion of shame, which implies the potential of being ostracized by the group. "Shame stimulates behaviour that leads to acceptance by the group, in addition to stimulating behaviour that flees group rejection; agreeing with the group norm is one of these behaviours" (Frijda & Mesquita 1994:78).

So if you wanted to belong to Israel, and in the process protect the group and your family honor, you had better communicate that identity in the proper way as established by the norms of the broader community and so help to preserve the integrity and boundary of the community as well. Think back to the period before the onset of the Maccabean revolt and the introduction of a gymnasium in Jerusalem. Those Israelite males who performed an epispasm to participate in the novelty were said to have forsaken the "holy covenant" (1 Macc 1:15). This was an accusation that said they have not only turned their backs on God, but also on what their co-ethnics expected of them, and as a result, they betrayed their ethnic identity. *Psalm of Solomon* 17:15 similarly laments that "the children of the covenant" living among "Gentile rabble" adopted foreign customs. As the author perceives the situation, the cultural differentiation of the Israelite people is under threat. Apostle Paul was seen as posing a similar threat. According to Luke when Paul was in Jerusalem believers were told "that you teach all the Judeans who live among the Gentiles to turn away from Moses, telling them not to circumcise their children or live according to our customs" (Acts 21:21), and later Paul was accused of bringing Greeks into the temple (v. 28). The Johannine community is warned: "They will put you out of the assembly/synagogue" (John 16:2), so evidently were not seen as communicating Israelite identity in the proper way, and indeed, undermined that identity, and so had to face expulsion from the Israelite community.

4. *Ethnicity is concerned with culture—shared meaning.*

To begin with, groups of people have their own value systems, which in collectivist societies members are expected to share. Important values for Israelites were God/Yahweh (monotheism), their divine election, the covenant relationship with God and his gift of the Torah, their shared ancestry and history, as well as the promise of their deliverance and the reconstitution of an independent Israel (millennialism). More on this will be said in chapter 2. In relation to these values are particular cultural features that ethnicity theory has identified as important for ethnic identity. These include:

1. *name*, a corporate name that identifies the group;
2. *myths of common ancestry*, the group claims to be descendents of a particular person or group/family;
3. *shared "historical" memories*, the group points to common heroes and events of the past;
4. *land*, the group has actual or symbolic attachment to an ancestral land;
5. *language*, or local dialect;
6. *kinship*, members of the group belong to family units which in turn, demonstrate communal solidarity with the local community or tribe, and with the group as a national entity;
7. *customs* identifiable with that group;
8. *religion;* and
9. *phenotypical features*, which points to genetic features.

   (cf. Duling 2005:127–28; Esler 2003a:43–44)

Not all of these features, however, are needed for a particular ethnic group. The most widespread of these are kinship relations and myths of common ancestry. A connection to an ancestral land is also recognized as a primary cultural feature (Duling 2005:127; cf. Esler 2003a:44). Hall (2002:9–10) regards the three features listed here, along with a shared history, as "core elements" which determine membership in an ethnic group.

An Introduction to Ethnicity Theory

Miller (2008:175) takes "perceived common ancestry" as the distinctive feature of ethnic identity, as the other features can be applied to collectivities other than ethnic groups. More will be said about these cultural features in chapter 2, as we will explore how they contributed to shape a world of shared meaning for the Israelites.

Are these cultural features found in ancient texts? Here follows a few quotations from antiquity which indicate that a similar understanding of culture was present. First is a quotation from Herodotus:

> For there are many great reasons why we [i.e., those in Greece] should not do this [i.e., desert to the Persians], even if we so desired; first and foremost, the burning and destruction of the adornments and temples of our gods [*religion*], whom we have constrained to avenge to the utmost rather than make pacts with the perpetrator of these things, and next the kinship of all Greeks in blood and speech [*name, kinship, phenotypical features* and *myths of common ancestry* (?), *language*], and the shrines of gods and the sacrifices that we have in common [*religion*, with *shared "historical" memories* inferred], and the likeness of our way of life [*customs*], to all of which it would not befit the Athenians [*land* (?)] to be false. (*Hist.* 8.144)

Tacitus, the Roman historian, mentions that during the Roman war with Germany, the Germans debated the advantages of fighting or surrendering. To fight was to remember the "claims of fatherland [*land, kinship* implied], of ancestral freedom [*myths of common ancestry, shared "historical" memories*], of the gods of the homes of Germany [*name*], of the mother who shared his [i.e., Arminius; a German chieftain] prayers [*religion*], that Flavus [Arminius' brother, who was cooperating with the Romans] might not choose to be the deserter and betrayer rather than the ruler of his kinsfolk and relatives, and indeed of his own people [*kinship*]" (*Ann.* 2.10).

In the *Histories*, Tacitus writes again about a German tribe called the Tencteri who sent messengers to the Ubii tribe, now a Roman colony called Agripinenses and situated on the other side of the Rhine (cf. *Germ.* 28), with the following request:

> For your return into the unity of the German nation [*kinship*] and *name* we give thanks to the Gods whom we worship in common [*religion*] ... Let it be lawful for us to inhabit both banks of the Rhine, as it was of old for our ancestors [*land, myths of common*

> *ancestry, shared "historical" memories*] ... Resume the manners and *customs* of your *country*, renouncing the pleasures, through which ... the Romans secure their power against subject nations. A pure and untainted race, forgetting your past bondage, you will be the equals of all, or will even rule over others. (*Hist.* 4.64)

In their response, the people of Agripinenses speak of being united "with you and the other Germans, our kinsmen by blood."

Another text comes from the geographer Strabo: "For the *ethnos* of the Armenians and that of the Syrians and Arabians betray a close affinity, not only in their *language*, but in their mode of life [*customs*], and in their bodily build [*phenotypical features*], and particularly wherever they live as close neighbours [*land*]" (*Geography* 1.2.34). And our last text comes from the Tanak: He also said, "Blessed be the LORD, the God of Shem! [*religion*] May Canaan be the slave of Shem ... These are the sons of Shem [*myths of common ancestry*] by their clans [*kinship*] and *languages*, in their territories [*land*] and nations (*ethnesin*) (Gen 9:26; 10:31, NIV).

We can see that the cultural features listed above are represented in ancient literature. In fact, simply having these features in mind when reading the Tanak or other Israelite literature will produce an abundant harvest of relevant examples as the various texts already cited in this chapter amply demonstrate.

5. *Ethnicity is no more fixed than the culture of which it is a component*, or the situations in which it is produced and reproduced.

As the predominant approach to ethnicity theory informs us, ethnicity is something that is socially (re)constructed. It is subject to change, is freely chosen, and is not "fixed" or "natural." Duling (2005:127) also points out, however, that although most theorists agree that people ascribe their ethnicity to themselves (constructionism), there is still great interest in the "cultural stuff." There is also still wide disagreement on whether self-constructed ethnicity is "irrational and ineffable" (primordialist) or "rational and self-interested" (instrumentalist). Apart from the psychological and emotional dynamics, this debate also brings into focus whether ethnicity is more fluid and changing, or on the other hand, a more "fixed" phenomenon.

Constructionism was largely formulated in response and in opposition to what is known as "primordialism," associated with the work of Edward Shils (1957a; 1957b) and Clifford Geertz (1963). Primordialism has traditionally been accused in that it sees ethnicity as something "natural," "pre-social," or "fixed," hence the opposite claims of constructionism outlined above. So what does primordialism actually involve? At the basic level it describes that "ethnic groups are held together by 'natural affections.' These are bonds so compelling, so passionate, so 'coercive,' and so overpowering, that they are fixed, *a priori*, involuntary, ineffable, even as 'sacred.' These bonds are deeply rooted in family, territory, language, custom, and religion" (Duling 2005:126). They are, in a word, "primordial."[11] In this instance one's ethnic identity "may not be so much a matter of choice, still less rational choice, but of tradition and emotions provoked by a common ancestry" (Esler 2003a:45). But it is important to mention that what Shils and Geertz described is what these primordial attachments are like for the social actors themselves (cf. Scott 1990:150; Fenton 2003:80–84). Jenkins explains that Geertz recognizes the role that culture plays in defining primordial bonds and that it varies in intensity in different societies and different time periods. Further, for Geertz "what matters analytically is that ties of blood, language and culture are *seen* by actors to be ineffable and obligatory; that they are *seen* as natural" (Jenkins 1997:45; emphasis original).

There have been attempts to argue away the merits of primordialism (Eller & Coughlan 1993; Denzey 2002), yet it needs to be taken into consideration for several reasons. First, it is a form of cognition, a result of the basic mental process of (social) categorization. Ethnicity provides an easy and reliable mental map making the world more predictable and gives apparently fixed distinctions between groups. It subconsciously governs expectations such as from whom can I expect danger or help and support? Who do I treat as one of my own, or as an outsider? (Suny 2001:893).

Second, it is about human beings being influenced by their immediate environment. We are dealing here with the effects of enculturation and socialization leading to habitual dispositions (*habitus*), and being part of the "plausibility system." Fenton (2003:89–90) also points out that

> to "think out of existence" primordiality is somehow to turn one's back on affect, the powerful influence of familiarity and customariness in social life, and the diffuse sense of attachment that flows

---

11. Fenton (2003:83) points out, however, that neither Shils nor Geertz themselves were defining *ethnicity*. They merely pointed out that some relationships (family, religion, language, customs etc) had a distinctive—primordial—quality when compared with others, such as your relationship with the state.

> from circumstances of birth and socialization, use of language and ingrained habits of thought and social practice ... It is simply to acknowledge that this kind of familiarity exists, that habits of thought do become ingrained and are often associated with early life, place, the family, and wider grouping or regions.

Again emphasis must be placed on the role of the family or kinship patterns in identity formation, and particularly in a context where ethnic differentiation is prominent (Jenkins 1997:47, 58–59).[12]

Third, it is how the social actors themselves could perceive the nature of their identity. Human beings attempt to make sense of the world, give meaning to their world, and finding their own place or identity within it. Primordial attachments, apart from being a matter of habit and familiarity, concern the stuff of history, faithfulness to tradition, a shared destiny, honour, and a sense of belonging to a community (cf. Scott 1990:163; Grosby 1996:55).

What is proposed here is that when we deal with first-century Israel we are dealing with primordial identity construction (cf. Suny 2001). The implication is that we need to see their identity as more "fixed" than "fluid." The motivation for this argument is that although Israelite ethnicity was socially (re)constructed, in its "essence" it was primordialist in nature, meaning that Israelites had strong psychological, emotional or "primordial attachment" to aspects of their identity, relevant to those living in Palestine as well as the diaspora.[13] In their own language it can be described as "zeal."[14] As this book invites the reader to put on Israelite sandals, to take a mental journey into their way of seeing the world, the social-scientific category of primordialism will help us in this process.

---

12. Jenkins, however, avoids using the term "primordial." Where ethnic identity is sufficiently salient to be internalized during early primary socialization, ethnicity can be characterized as a *primary*—not primordial—dimension of individual identity (Jenkins 1997:47).

13. Diaspora Israelites would have been ethnic minorities wherever they lived, and often lived in the same areas of the city. This social scenario runs contrary to the notion that they were not Torah obedient (cf. Trebilco 1991:12–36, 187–89). Esler (2003a:64–66) also pints out that Judeans in the Diaspora had to work harder to maintain their distinctive identity and would have maintained a strong attachment to the temple in Jerusalem and the law in the synagogue.

14. Cf. Phil 3:6; Gal 1:13–14 (on Paul); Gen 34; Jdt 9:2–4; *Jub.* 30 (on Simeon and Levi); Num 11:29; 25:6–13; Sir 45:23–24; 1 Macc 2:54; *4 Macc* 18:12 (on Phinehas); 1 Kgs 18; Sir 48:2–3; 1 Macc 2:58 (on Elijah); 1 Macc 2:23–27; Josephus *Ant.* 12.271; 2 Macc 4:2 (on the Maccabees) (see Dunn 2008:12 et al).

And although this approach emphasizes the view of the participant, or how ethnic groups themselves understand reality (i.e. an insider or emic perspective), from an etic (or outsider) perspective primordialism brings to attention the emotional and psychological strength of ethnic affiliation, why it exists, and how it came to be that way. So our aim is neither to endorse nor to condemn, but to understand these strangers and how they survived the attraction of cultural assimilation.

In the world of the New Testament change or deviant behavior was not seen as a good thing and deviant behavior in particular was generally seen as shameful. It questioned both the value of and loyalty to ancestral tradition. The culture of the time valued stability and constancy of character and compliance, and the willingness to conform one's actions to cultural standards. These attitudes are more typical of agricultural and highly stratified societies of which ancient Israel is a clear example. More impetus to resist change came from the foundational belief to live in conformity with God's changeless Law (Malina & Neyrey 1996:39; McVann 1993a; 1993b; Berry et al. 2002:56–59). Adherence to the law, custom and tradition was therefore a measure by which you could be judged as an honorable person. According to Ben Sirach (10:19–24), honour was to be found in obedience to God and the Torah (= wisdom) and following the values of Israelite culture (Jewett 2003; DeSilva 1996). Mattathias likewise exhorted his sons: "[B]e zealous for the law, and give your lives for the covenant of your fathers. Call to remembrance what acts our fathers did in their time; so you will receive great honour and an everlasting name" (1 Macc 2:50–51). Other Israelite texts explain that to renounce the Law is to abandon ancestral beliefs (*3 Macc* 1:3; *4 Macc* 16:16), or the customs of the fathers (*2 Macc* 11:25; *4 Macc* 18:5). Eleazar, at the time of the Maccabean revolt, is said to have exclaimed: "I will not violate the solemn oaths of my ancestors to keep the Law, not even if you gouge out my eyes and burn my entrails" (*4 Macc* 5:29; cf. 9:1–2, 29). Israel is admonished: "O offspring of the seed of Abraham, children of Israel, obey this Law and be altogether true to your religion" (*4 Macc* 18:1). Daniel supposedly said: "Far be it from me to leave the heritage of my fathers and cleave to the inheritances of the uncircumcised" (*Liv. Pro.* 4:16). In 1 and 2 Enoch the following texts are found:

> Woe to you who reject the foundations and the eternal inheritance of your forefathers! (*1 En.* 99:14)

> Happy—who preserves the foundations of his most ancient fathers, made firm from the beginning. Cursed—he who breaks down the institutions of his ancestors and fathers. (*2 En.* 52:9–10 [J])[15]

Israelites lived in what has been called a "high context society," where there is very little social change over time. Contextual knowledge was assumed, widely shared and known, and need not be explained in written or oral communication (Rohrbaugh 2007:8–10). This contextual knowledge can be equated to their world of meaning, which helped to shape the *habitus*. So performing covenantal praxis or "works of the law," embodying as it were various primordial attachments, was to remain true to ancestral traditions, being obedient to God and his law, participating in a world of shared meaning, maintaining your family and collective honor, as well as the relationship and inter-dependence with significant others. Overall, it was being faithful to your Israelite ethnic identity.

More reasons can be adduced for seeing Israelite ethnic identity as being primordialist in nature. Since the Israelites formed an often-despised minority in the Roman empire, their identity always came under threat through various means: through the lure of assimilation, acculturation, or active oppression. Primordial sentiments flourish in contexts of political suffocation and where there is a sense of political dismemberment. Human beings generally refuse to submit to another system in order not to submit to degradation. It is to refuse to be made out as a lesser order of being, as irrelevant, powerless, and simple-minded (Geertz 2000 [1973]:264, 276). We can just sympathize with Israelites thinking of their general experience under Rome. Primordial sentiments also become greater the greater the amount of *opposition* experienced by that group. Scott explains "with respect to the *content* of ethnic identity, the primordial sentiments will also attach to the symbols against which the greatest opposition is expressed, whether language, territory, heroes, music, dance, cuisine, or clothing, such that they will become even more salient in the individual's reckoning of his or her ethnicity" (Scott 1990:163; emphasis original). Think of the onslaught of Hellenism before the Maccabean revolt, and the policies of Antiochus IV Epiphanes that prohibited Israelite practices. Think of the attempts of the Emperor Gaius to have a statue of himself erected in the temple in Jerusalem. What about that maver-

---

15. On the honor and shame values expressed in reproaches (woes) and makarisms (beatitudes), see Hanson 1994[96].

ick Israelite Paul, who ate with "the Foreskins" (cf. Eph 2:11) and even made the preposterous claim that they have Abraham as forefather and are saved by Jesus Messiah *as Gentiles*! The Israelites also constantly requested the emperor or other rulers that they may practice their ancestral customs without interference, such as the right to assembly and observe the Sabbath, and to send the temple tax to Jerusalem. Decrees were given for Judean men to be exempted from military service because it interfered with the requirements of the Sabbath and Israelite dietary regulations (Josephus *Ant.* 14.185ff.).

Depending on the needs of the situation, Israelites fought either violently or used diplomacy to preserve their identity and distinctiveness, in other words to observe the "customs of their fathers." It should come as no surprise that things such as circumcision, food and purity laws, and Sabbath observance would feature so prominently in the letters of Paul, where the identity of the Messianist community versus traditional Israelite identity was so hotly contested.

One must not confuse this with the idea of Israelites (especially those of the diaspora) forming totally isolated communities, or that they were not in various ways influenced by their surrounding culture. In some areas of social life interaction was forbidden, while in others it was allowed (cf. Esler 1998:87). For alongside the process of *dis*simulation would have occurred cultural and structural *as*similation.[16] We can, among other things, mention how the Israelites were influenced by Hellenistic forms of architecture, government, literature and language, as well as notions of the afterlife (cf. Cromhout 2007:123–47). Cohen (1993:3) also contends that apart from the hidden reality of circumcision, "Jews" of antiquity were vi-

---

16. According to Harland (2003:196), *cultural assimilation* (or acculturation) "can involve the selection, adoption, and adaptation of a variety of cultural traits including language, dress, religion, and other cultural conventions, beliefs, and values that make up the way of life and worldview of a particular group." Some elements are accepted, yet undergoes transformation, while others are rejected. "At both the individual and group levels acculturation need not be substitutive, replacing a set of cultural traits or radically changing worldview; rather it can be additive, allowing for the continuation of a particular individual's or group's identity and cultural framework despite acculturation." *Structural assimilation* occurs on two levels. At the primary level, "individual members of a given ethnic or cultural group can interact with persons from other cultural groups through personal social network connections, including memberships in neighbourhoods, clubs, and associations . . . The secondary level of structural assimilation involves members of a particular cultural group becoming more evident and participatory in the formal political, legal, social, or economic institutions of society" (2003:197).

sually indistinguishable from their neighbors. "Not a single ancient author says that the Jews are distinctive because of their looks, clothing, speech, names, or occupation." Harland (2003:200–12, 227–28; cf. Lieu 2002:31–47) explains that Judeans (he calls them "Jews") participated in civic life and the *polis* in various ways. First, there is participation in the central socio-cultural institutions of the *polis*, such as the theatre and activities of the gymnasium; and Judeans would form age-group associations or join ones that already existed. Second, some Judean groups also took part in the civic networks of benefaction. For example, Josephus mentions a decree made in Sardis, which provided the Judeans a place to meet (*Ant.* 14.259–61). Julia Severa, an imperial cult high priestess, appears to have contributed a building to the Judeans of Akmoneia around 60–80 CE. Third, there are connections with other subgroups for social or business purposes. Philo's writings suggest that Judeans joined local guilds or associations in the cities (*Embassy* 3.155–59; *Drunkeness* 20–26).

6. *Ethnicity is both collective and individual*, externalized in social interaction and internalized in personal self-identification.

As mentioned already, ethnicity is something in a person's head, whether that of the social actor in question or the observer. Yet it is also externalized in "objective" social reality. Groups can be and are identified based on common interests or behavioral characteristics, such as the way they speak or dress. Ethnic identity is no different. The bonds that hold Israelites together were social, thus established through their observance of ancestral customs (Barclay 1996:209). Ethnicity is a social activity (Hall 1997:25). In other words, it was externalized in social interaction through which relationships with significant others, and as a result, collective identity was maintained.

Being an Israelite, one obvious example of how collective identity came to expression was through participation in pilgrimage festivals. Both Josephus (*Ant.* 4.203–4) and Philo (*SpecLaws* 1.70) testify to the sense of community that they create. There would be the gatherings in the synagogue or assemblies on the Sabbath. There would also be the day-to-day tasks of preparing food according to the laws of *kashrut* (food laws), denoting food that is fit for consumption, and celebrating common meals, such as the "pure supper" (*cena pura* or *prosabbaton*), which in the diaspora denoted a communal dinner before the onset of the Sabbath (Horbury 2006). Pilgrimage festivals also occasioned feasting, and food and meals are "highly complex social events utilized to reinforce social values, boundaries, statuses, and hierarchies" (Neufeld 2000:16). Participation in meals communicated who belonged to your social world, and created communal solidarity and social cohesion (cf. Philo *SpecLaws* 1.221; Josephus *Ant.* 4.7). There would be working the God-given land, since most first-century Israelites were peasants working their land for subsistence, a way of life that came under serious threat through indebtedness and exploitation (Fiensy 1991; Oakman 2008).

Ethnicity is also internalized in personal self-identification. Above we already discussed the role of socialization, and how social actors receive specific instruction in order to become competent participants in their ethnic group. This goes hand in hand with the inherent tendency for people to categorize themselves into social groups. Jenkins mentions that the "sense of self," located in the *habitus*, is much influenced by categorization, a process that occurs already during childhood. "Entering into ethnic identification during childhood is definitively a matter of categorization: we learn who we are because, in the first instance, other people—whether they be co-members or Others—tell us. Socialization *is* categorization" (Jenkins 1997:166; emphasis original). Where ethnicity is important, a child will not only learn she is an "X," but also what it means: "in terms of her esteem and worth in her own eyes and in the eyes of others; in terms of appropriate and inappropriate behaviour; and in terms of what it means *not* to be an 'X' . . ." (Jenkins 1997:59; emphasis original). So how you perceive yourself has to do with the cognitive, evaluative, and emotional dimensions of group membership already outlined earlier. You categorize yourself and others into groups. You exaggerate similarities and differences. You attach a value to your group membership, form stereotypes and expectations, and exercise loyalty and cooperate with your own group.

One can see how the process of categorization would be relevant to collectivist societies, where the individual would normally see himself or herself through the eyes of others. Here individuals are group-orientated personalities. The "dyadic" person is essentially a "group-embedded and group-orientated person . . . Such persons internalize and make their own what others say, do, and think about them because they believe it is necessary, for being human, to live out the expectation of others" (Malina 1993:67). Important is the interaction between the individual and "person-sustaining groups" such as the family, village or city, and nation.

So importantly, if you were an Israelite living in the first century the content and meaning of your "sense of self" was largely determined by the group you belonged to. "Who am I?" would not have been answered in individualistic terms. The answer would have been something as follows: "Look at the group I belong to. This is who I am." Their self-awareness and self-definition depended upon the group within which they were embedded (cf. Malina & Neyrey 2008). And along with this would be the normative requirement to measure up to the cultural expectations or stereotypes associated with that identity.

Hopefully the reader will now be more familiar with the dynamics of ethnic identity. To briefly summarize, at the most fundamental level ethnicity is a form of cognition, the recognition that you belong to a group and claiming with it all its supposed advantages. It is how you view the world. It is a feeling of attachment and solidarity with a specific group of people. It is the way you came to see the world because of your upbringing and various sources of social interaction. It is about being similar to some people and at the same time being different to others. It is about living in a world of shared meaning. It is about responding or adapting to various social situations. It is about participating in a community's customs, mostly social activities, and making the self submerge as part of a collective. With this work behind us, we can move forward and refine our approach towards Israelite ethnic identity, something we will aim to achieve in the next chapter.

2

A Socio-Cultural Model of Israelite Ethnicity

WE WANT TO WALK, as much as our imagination allows us, in Israelite sandals. In chapter 1 some of the most salient aspects of ethnicity were introduced and hopefully it served as a primer and invitation to achieve this end. With this theoretical foundation behind us, we can move forward and refine our approach to Israelite identity. The work that follows largely draws from chapter 2 of *Jesus and Identity: Reconstructing Judean ethnicity in Q* (Cromhout 2007) where a Socio-Cultural Model of Judean Ethnicity was developed. But here we will make a few additions, some minor modifications, and of course, we will incorporate the model developed and explained in chapter 1 as well.

The Socio-Cultural Model of Judean Ethnicity previously developed was a hybrid of various theological and social-scientific approaches. Firstly, it incorporated the insights of Sanders (1977; 1992), and his formulation of "covenantal nomism," which correctly questioned the existing paradigm where "Judaism" was made a caricature, seen as a "religion" of merit, where Israelites were seen as always struggling along trying to "earn" their way to salvation through "works." What Sanders demonstrated was that the literature testifies to a pattern of religion where Israelites were seen as already in the covenant. Their call was to *remain* within the covenant. As "covenantal nomism" attempts to capture, it is about "getting in" (already accomplished: God elected Israel and gave them his law) and "staying in" (through obedience to the law and atonement) the covenant. Despite apparent attempts to the contrary, "covenantal nomism," although an etic description, remains to be a useful way to capture the essence of Israelite self-understanding (cf. the contributions in Carson, O'Brien & Seifrid 2001). At the same time, however, "covenantal nomism" was adapted to serve as an *ethnic*—not religious—descriptor which may be summarized as follows: "God called a particular people and in that process established a constitution or charter (= covenant as expressed through the Torah) of Judean ethnic identity. The people elected must respond to that call, and so give expression to that ethnic identity through obedience to the constitution. Differently put, God established Judean ethnic identity. A group of people respond(ed) by being Judean, in whatever way was deemed necessary" (Cromhout 2007:69). The focus therefore shifts to understanding Judeans/Israelites as living out their ethnic identity, thus created and maintained within the orbit of the covenant, which at the same time necessitates a different and more fruitful means by which to approach aspects of biblical interpretation. It is to come to terms with the Israelite people as a socio-cultural reality, and not merely approaching them as a people with a particular "theology."

Second, the model utilized Dunn's "four pillars of Second Temple Judaism," which include the Temple, God, Election, and Torah, as well as the New Perspective on Paul (NPP) (Dunn 1990; 1991; 2003). The four pillars, so Dunn argues, established a common foundation of belief and practice for Israelites. As shall be explained later, these pillars have variously to do with both the core values, as well as the more visible aspects of Israelite identity. In itself the NPP brings attention to the social and ethnic dimensions of Israelite identity, especially in its interaction with the Gentile world, and with the help of ethnicity theory the insights of the NPP can be developed even further.

Third—the main inspiration for the model—I utilized the Socio-Cultural Model of Ethnicity developed by Duling (2005). His model lists key representative socio-cultural features that could influence an ethnic group's values, norms, and behavior (reflected in point 4 of the model discussed in chapter 1). He describes it as an outsider's model (etic model) that is "imposed" on the available data, a "socio-cultural umbrella" that highlights "cultural stuff," while also reflecting the dominant constructionist approach in ethnicity theory reflected in the broken lines. Duling's model is visualized on the opposite page.

Fourth, the model also made use of Berger & Luckmann (1967) and their sociological construct known as the "symbolic universe." Their approach will help us to understand that Israelites and their Judean way of life was a way of being and knowing, the way they understood their "world," which provided an interconnected tapestry of meaning as well as legitimation for how they lived and how they related to others. It is particularly on this feature we will now concentrate in order to power our

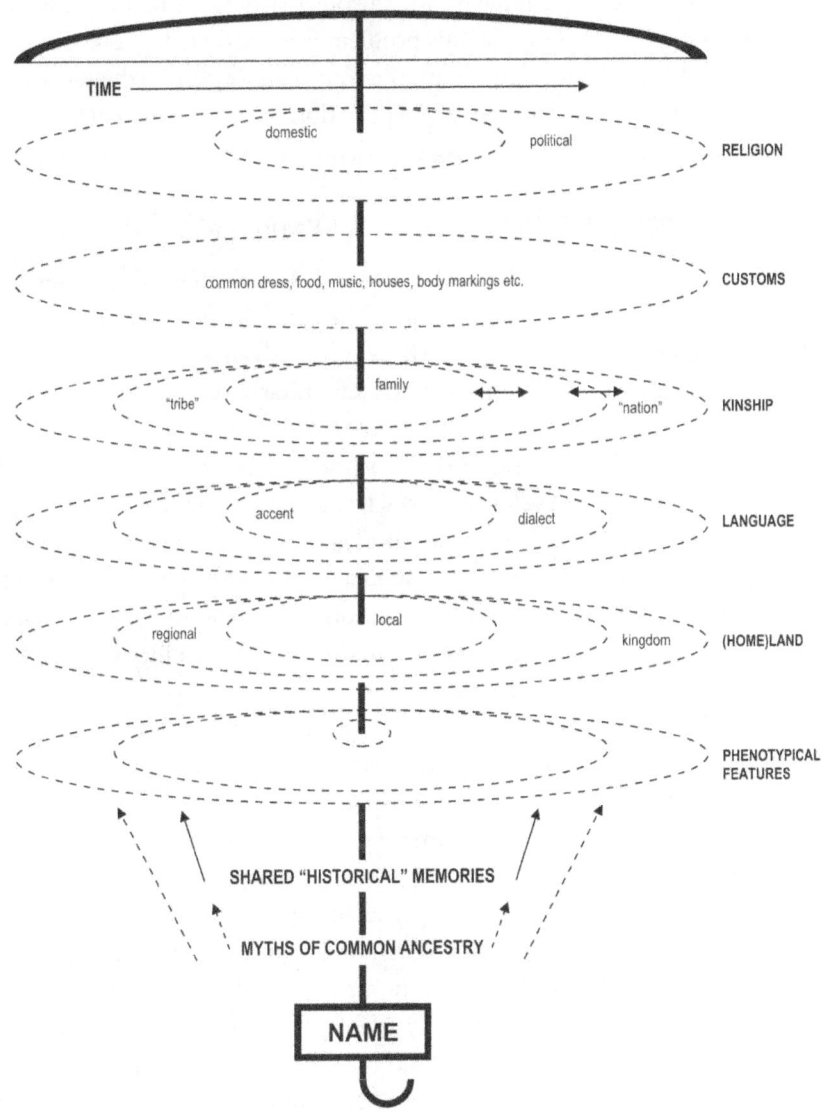

D C Duling's Socio-Cultural Model of Ethnicity

imagination, that is, for the purpose of our mental journey into a strange universe, to walk in Israelite sandals. We will never garner a complete understanding of their universe for various reasons, the main one being we are "outsiders" looking in. This problem is exacerbated by our distance in time and the limited information at our disposal. Nevertheless, what we can attempt to achieve is to have a peak through the somewhat blurry window, look inside, and see if we can identify some characteristic features.

ISRAELITES LIVING IN A SYMBOLIC UNIVERSE

Think about your own place in the world. As you grew up and found your place within it, some things seemed "natural" to you. They have "always" been there, or due to rapid technological advancements there is always new gadgets and inventions you must familiarize yourself with. To use the internet, e-mail, iPod, and remote control for the TV is second nature. We are immersed in a world of media vying for our attention (and money!). If you live in the developed world, transport is generally easy and accessible, and distant regions of the world is an airplane ticket (and visa) away. From your home or office you can in a virtual sense "go to" any part of the world and be entertained by international news and sporting events. On a larger scale, you live in an ever expanding universe, billions of light-years across having its origin in a big bang.

Your own home was a place of various textures, customs, smells, and sounds. What food did you eat? Was it related to religious or cultural festivities? Was fast food available around the corner? The meat that you ate, was it neatly packaged in a supermarket, or did you slaughter the animal yourself? Were you encouraged to be independent or to conform to the norms and values of the group you belonged to? Did you choose your wife/husband or was this arranged by your parents? Was there a strict social order and hierarchy in your home or local community? Was your life governed by personal choices, by fate, or the expectations of the collective you belonged to? Did you attend a local church? Did you make sacrifices to your ancestors? Was your relationship with the divine or spiritual about eternal salvation, or about the quality of your life here and now? Is there life after death? Will you go to your ancestors or to heaven? Did you have water on tap and electricity in your home? Was nature something to be controlled, or something to be respected and feared? What kind of government or religious leadership did you have? Whatever your circumstances, you in a sense entered a world not of your own making. A social order existed which you discovered and adapted to. Yet this was the result of previous generations and their social interaction, a human production, itself a part of the ongoing process of human externalization.

Berger & Luckmann (1967:60) suggest that all human activity is subject to habitualization. Habitualized actions produce institutions, which typify both individual actors and individual actions. These various institutions form "knowledge" that are passed on from generation to generation and acquire an objective quality. In other words, it becomes the social construction of reality. Berger & Luckmann (1967:61) also explain "that the relationship between man, the producer, and the social world, his product, is and remains a dialectical one . . . The product acts back upon the producer." Thus externalization and objectification is followed by internalization. *"Society is a human product. Society is an objective reality. Man is a social product"* (Berger & Luckmann 1967:61; emphasis original; cf. Berger 1973:14). Recall from the previous chapter what was said about socialization and enculturation, and the formation of "habitual dispositions" (*habitus*), which shape and are shaped by cultural practises. Culture or "knowledge" is something that exists, something we are socialized into, internalize, and then also reproduce ourselves, and so is passed on from generation to generation.

For example, if you were born in Africa you were typically socialized into a world or set of knowledge of "groupness" (kinship), where your individual identity is derived from the collective identity, and where your individual self basically "disappears," being subordinate and answerable to the requirements of the collective. You must be obedient, respect your elders, subject yourself to the social hierarchy, and "fit in." Your ancestors and other spirits also formed part of your world impacting every aspect of your life, and by utilizing the means of various rituals you communicated with or obtained blessings from them. The ancestors would be held in high esteem, venerated, and seen as guarantors and models for group behavior and for the group's survival. To "sin" would be to do anything which disturbed social harmony within your group (not so much what I do in private), or would offend the ancestors by neglecting to perform a ritual, or by not remembering them. This sense of inter-relationships or inter-connectedness is so strong, that if something bad happens to you, like losing your job or getting ill, you would ask: *Who* did this to me? Have I offended somebody? Was I perhaps the victim of witchcraft?

Circumstances that come your way always have their root in *someone*, a person, an enemy, a witch, a spirit, or ancestor.

If you grew up in Northern Europe or America, you were typically socialized into a very different looking reservoir of "knowledge." You can be anything you want to be. You can express your "uniqueness." You are brought up to be independent and follow your ambition. Models of behavior were music groups and movie stars, influencing the way you dressed or your hairstyle, even the way you speak. Important is the search for "truth," individual freedom, and speaking your mind on anything. You are entitled to an opinion, no matter who you are. And if you attended your local church you learnt that "sin" is something committed against God, and can even occur in private, even in your thoughts. If you became ill, it was due to a virus or bacterial infection, or other scientific causes. You took pills and underwent blood tests and x-rays. You did not go to see a local shaman to help restore your relationships with significant others whom you perhaps offended, or to find out from him/her who caused your misfortune, or get some magical potion or amulet to counteract witchcraft.

In a similar way the people in the New Testament world had their own kind of "knowledge," different ways of understanding the world, just as there is also a plurality of worldviews in existence today (cf. Malina 1993; Esler 2000; Rohrbaugh 2007; Craffert 2007). This should make Bible reading, especially for Westerners, a task that should be approached with caution and modesty. In fact, the average person in Africa today would make for a better equiped Bible reader, for (s)he shares so many social values with the biblical world (Botha 2007), and would fill in the "missing cues" or contextual knowledge far more accurately. If we read the contrast outlined above we will see that African people share with the biblical world the emphasis on "groupness" and inter-personal relationships, obedience, the loyalty to past tradition and ancestors, as well as the understanding of where misfortune comes from (some*one*, not some*thing*).

Apart from these but few examples, what would have been typical of Israelite "knowledge"? Some of this "knowledge" was already introduced in chapter 1, but to answer this question in further detail we would also need to draw attention to some of the principal social institutions and values of the Mediterranean world in antiquity.

A Socio-Cultural Model of Israelite Ethnicity

Kinship

First of all, your world would be dominated by the institution of kinship. This was the primary realm of socialization and enculturation, the source of your identity, and the base of economic support. Being socialized into a collectivist society, everything revolved around their dependence and relationship to various social groups. The immediate family was normally the primary focus of activity and loyalty and available resources had to be used for its preservation. And it is where strong family groups exist where a social phenomenon such as ethnicity, a form of extended kinship, can develop in a most recognizable form. Horowitz (1985:55) points out that ethnic groups consist mostly of those who have been born into them—hence the importance of kinship or the family in the existence of ethnic groups. In other words, "a strong sense of ethnic identity is difficult to maintain without strong family ties" (1985:61). This goes hand-in-hand with endogamous marriage strategies, that is, where there was a high expectation of marriage between close kin. This is why ethnic affiliations have generally greater power and are more pervasive in areas such as Africa and Asia than in the West. For first-century Israelites, endogamous marriage was part of a "defensive" marriage strategy, to protect their ethnic boundaries and to produce "holy seed" (Jdt 8:2; Tob 1:9; 3:15–17; 4:12–13; *Jub.* 30:7–8) (Hanson 1996:70; Malina 1993:129–38). This strategy had its roots in the post-exilic priestly reformation of Ezra and Nehemiah (Nehemiah 9–10; Ezra 9–10). "Holy seed" refers to a people who are ritually pure, holy, headed by priests and with worship centered on the temple. They are people who have a pure Israelite ancestry, not tainted by mixed offspring and sexual relations with Gentiles, and so whose ethnic identity was intact, protected, and preserved.

The family for Israelites was patriarchal, where the father (*paterfamilias*) stood as the supreme head and provided the central axis for unity. The family was also patrilineal, as identity and social status was transmitted from father to son in successive generations (Guijarro 2001). It therefore also became a matter of asking: Who were my ancestors? Having a certain ancestry or genealogy entitled a person or family to certain roles and statuses, determined suitable marriage partners (e.g., Deut 7:1–4), and what functions you could perform (e.g., being a priest) (Hanson 1994; 1996; 2008).

Honor and Shame

The institution of kinship is closely interlinked with the primary values of honor and shame. Belonging to a kinship group determined your honor ranking within society. By implication, being part of a kinship group meant you had to contribute towards protecting the family honor. Honor was making the claim to having a certain social standing ("worth"), and having that claim acknowledged by society. This social standing was something continually contested in the game of challenge and riposte, and if you gained honor, the group benefitted from it also. Honor was also associated with the wealth of a family. Alternatively, honor was measured within Israel by obedience to the law (Sir 10:19–24).

To be in a state of shame is to lack or lose honor, to lose social standing, which may or may not include the loss of family wealth. To "have shame," however, also refers to the positive function of protecting family honor and to be sensitive to the opinion of others, otherwise you would be "shameless." It was in particular the duty of unmarried women to protect their shame (the female version of protecting their "honor"), by taking care of their virginity and chastity, otherwise they would destroy the honor of their families, particularly that of its male members (*Jub.* 20:4) (cf. Moxnes 1996; Malina & Rohrbaugh 1992:76–77; Marohl 2008; Neyrey 2008).

What is of particular interest to us here is the notion of "ascribed honor," that is, honor derived through descent or as a grant from an honorable person. In discussing the *progymnasmata* and physiognomic writings, Malina & Neyrey (1996) identified three important status markers in antiquity: generation, geography, and gender. Particularly generation and geography are important for our purposes here, as they help to explain how kinship, ethnic identity, and ascribed honor are interrelated. The elements of the status markers are set out as follows:

A Socio-Cultural Model of Israelite Ethnicity

Ascribed honor:

Generation

   Individual
1. physical attributed: beauty, strength, agility, might, health
2. physiognomic features
3. native intelligence
4. age

   Group
5. <u>immediate family: parentage, especially father</u>
6. <u>ancestors; genealogies</u>
7. <u>tribe, clan, or *ethnos*</u>
8. <u>language; speech; dialect</u>

Geography
9. <u>city of origin</u>
10. <u>region of origin</u>

Gender

The underlined points have direct bearing on ethnic identity (Duling 2008a:808–9). Most immediately your honor ranking was determined by your parents, particularly your father, which extends back to his lineage, and wider through belonging to a tribe or *ethnos*, which in the ancient world was predictably associated with an ancestral territory and stereotypical characteristics expected of its people. All Israelites, of course, would have traced their ancestries back to the patriarchs and those who settled the land at the time of the Exodus. As far as the Israelites were concerned, they belonged to an honorable people, indeed, the most worthy of honor, as they understood themselves to be "a chosen and honored race from the seed of Jacob" (*T. Job* 1:5). As already mentioned in the previous chapter they would have seen themselves as a special people, as the objects of divine favour. The world was created by their God, who established a special relationship with them stretching back to Abraham, Isaac, and Jacob. Israel is the "portion and inheritance of God" (*Pss. Sol.* 14:5), and elsewhere the *Psalms of Solomon* makes the following plea:

> And now, you are God and we are the people whom you have loved; look and be compassionate, O God of Israel, for we are yours, and do not take away your mercy from us, lest they set upon us. For you chose the descendants of Abraham above all the nations, and

you put your name upon us, Lord, and it will not cease forever. You made a covenant with our ancestors concerning us, and we hope in you when we turn our souls toward you. May the mercy of the Lord be upon the house of Israel forevermore. (*Pss. Sol.* 9:8–11)

Patronage and Clientage

Apart from belonging to an honorable people and having a privileged ancestry, one other aspect important to the world of Israelites would be their relationship to their ancestral land. This affects another important institution of antiquity, namely, that of patronage and clientage, which worked as follows. It consisted of reciprocal relationships between social unequals. Patrons, people of higher social status, were those who controlled resources and were expected to grant favours to clients (also cities and villages). Clients on the other hand, were people of lower social status and dependent on the generosity of patrons to survive in society. They were expected to return the patron's favor in whatever way was deemed necessary, to give their loyalty, and to give them public honors. Between the patrons and clients you had "brokers," and the more clients a patron had, the higher was his or her social status (Malina & Rohrbaugh 1992:74–76).

In a similar fashion Yahweh was the patron of Israel. He gave them the covenant, the law, and the land. In return, the Israelites had to give him loyalty, honor (being the equivalent of "praise"), and sacrifices. Their God was the patron of patrons, and in return for their loyalty he provided blessing and protection (Malina 1993:170–71).

One of the most important favors granted to Israel was a special territory. The gift of the land was a primary reason for the existence of the covenant, and according to Brueggemann (2002), it is the *central theme* of biblical faith. The gift of the land goes hand-in-hand with the institution of kinship, as the land or family smallholdings were ideally passed on from generation to generation. The divine patron of course also provides food through the land, which demonstrates that the land was not merely a place to live, but was also the means of subsistence, thus, closely connected to the institution of *economics*. This way of living naturally focussed on Jerusalem and the temple, being regarded as the center of the world and place of pilgrimage (cf. Philo *Flaccus* 7.46; *Embassy* 36.281; *Providence* 2.64; *Jubilees* 8). The major pilgrimage festivals celebrated some or other aspect of agriculture, where in addition to celebrating God's acts of redemption in history, they afforded opportunities to bring various offerings as tokens of gratitude for God's generous provision through the land (Leviticus 16, 23; Deuteronomy 16). For most Israelites, life was about the seasonal planting and harvesting of crops, as agriculture was the principal economic activity of Israel and her households. In the first century this way of life came under severe threat, as exploitation and taxes, especially under Roman government, and other factors such as overpopulation and bad harvests resulted in debt, loss of land, and tenant farming (Fiensy 1991; Oakman 2008).

The gift of the land also meant living in a space that grounded your identity. However, Israelites lived in a state of cognitive dissonance as the gift of the land and all the benefits it entailed conflicted with reality, as they found themselves politically subordinated and formed part of the Roman Empire. This kind of frustrated relationship to the land extended back to the Exile, somewhat alleviated by the Hasmonean dynasty, but entrenched with the arrival of the Roman General Pompey who took control of Jerusalem and subsequently the entire region starting 63 BCE. In response to the Roman occupation the following call for freedom was made:

> See, Lord, and raise up for them their king ... Undergird him with the strength to destroy unrighteous rulers, to purge Jerusalem from gentiles who trample her to destruction ... He will gather a holy people ... He will distribute them upon the land according to their tribes; the alien and the foreigner will no longer live near them ... And he will have gentile nations serving him under his yoke ... And he will purge Jerusalem ... (for) nations to come from the ends of the earth to see his glory, to bring as gifts her children who had been driven out. (*Pss. Sol.* 16:21–31)

This hope for freedom characterized Israelites throughout this period and gave rise to various "messiah" and "prophet" figures promising redemption (Horsley 1987). Alas, any millennial hopes were repeatedly crushed, especially in the revolts of 66–70 and 132–135 CE, where Israelite identity had to be negotiated, indeed (re)constructed, as the temple was destroyed and any relationship to the land, especially Jerusalem, the *axis mundi* of the Judean way of life, made unbearingly remote. *Fourth Ezra*, for example, struggles with God, trying to make sense of the loss and devastation in light of the events in 70 CE. God is told: you "have destroyed your people, and have preserved your enemies . . . Are the deeds of Babylon [i.e., Rome] better than those of Zion? Or has another nation known you besides Israel? Or what tribes have so believed your covenants [cf. 5:29] as these tribes of Jacob." The other nations are nothing before God, but "we your people, who you have called your first-born, only begotten, zealous for you, and most dear, have been given into their hands. *If the world has indeed been created for us* [it was, according to 7:11], *why do we not possess our world as an inheritance?*" (4 Ezra 6:56–59).

Ethnic identity also encodes power relationships, that is, it can discriminate between ethnic groups who have power, privilege, prestige, honor, and those who are subordinated, those who have little access to resources, the exploited and humiliated. Israelite ethnic identity in the first century proved to be a way of seeing the world that had to negotiate between what ought to be and everyday reality. It ought to be honorable, blessed with God's patronage and benefaction, protection, with land, rich harvests, social justice, free of debt, and freedom to live the ancestral way of life. But what you see are Roman soldiers patrolling the roofs of the temple porticoes (Josephus *War* 2.224–27; *Ant.* 20.112), or worse, a destroyed temple and many Israelites crucified or taken into slavery (*War* 5.449; 6.420ff.). What you see are the founding of cities named after your imperial overlords, such as Tiberias or Caesarea. If you are a father, you see that your son has lost his inheritance (the land) because of debt. You see the corruption of the rich in Jerusalem, including the high priestly families, enriching themselves at the cost of traditional piety and the honor of peasant families (Josephus *Ant.* 20.180–81, 206–7; *b. Pes.* 57a). This is a rough summary of some of the circumstances during the first century CE, but the overall point is that the average Israelite peasant suffered under political, economic, and cultural suffocation. What else could they do but hope in their divine patron for deliverance and restore the order and balance of their universe?

Legitimation of "Knowledge"

Berger & Luckmann also explain that the institutional order or "knowledge" requires *legitimation* if it is to be transmitted to a new generation. "Legitimation not only tells the individual why he *should* perform one action and not another; it also tells him why things *are* what they are. In other words, 'knowledge' precedes 'values' in the legitimation of in-

A Socio-Cultural Model of Israelite Ethnicity

stitutions" (Berger & Luckmann 1967:94; emphasis original). A means of legitimation is where the entire institutional order is placed within a "symbolic universe." A symbolic universe is where "*all* the sectors of the institutional order are integrated in an all-embracing frame of reference, which now constitutes a universe in the literal sense of the word, because *all* human experience can now be conceived of as taking place *within* it. The symbolic universe is conceived of as the matrix of *all* socially objectivated and subjectively real meanings; the entire historic society and the entire biography of the individual are seen as events taking place *within* this universe" (Berger & Luckmann 1967:96; emphasis original).

If we transpose this insight and apply it to Israelites of the first century, their life was lived within a realm, a symbolic universe, with Yahweh (the divine patron) standing above all things, and his clients (the Israelites) living according to his law. Josephus speaks of the Israelites in the following way: "Unity and identity of religious belief, perfect uniformity in habits and customs, produce a very beautiful concord in human character." It is particularly the law that "above all we owe our admirable harmony . . . Among us alone will be heard no contradictory statements about God . . . among us alone will be seen no difference in the conduct of our lives. With us all act alike, all profess the same doctrine about God" (*Apion* 2.179–81).

All aspects of life were under God and should be lived in accordance with God's will (cf. *Apion* 2.170–73). In the very least, that was the ideal. But Josephus says in his own way that Israelites generally share the same "knowledge" and understanding of how the world should work, what people should do and why things are what they are. Their God/Patron wanted it that way (Deut 11:27–28)! And of course, this went hand-in-hand with preserving the honor of the ancestors and to emulate their example (Isa 51:1–2). It is only natural therefore that shared knowledge and culture is the equivalent of shared *meaning* ("truth"), and where we find shared meaning a shared *identity*, such as ethnic groups, can find an existence.

According to Fishman (1996:66, 68), ethnicity is a "*Weltanschauung* that helps to explain origins, clarify eternal questions, rationalize human destiny, and purports to offer an entre to universal truths . . . [Ethnicity] is an experience of deeply rooted, intimate and eternal belonging." The House of Israel can also be understood as a more "vertical" ethnic group, where "a single ethnic culture permeates in varying degrees most strata of the population" (Smith 1986:77). They can also be understood as a "totalizing ethnicity," where "ethnic organization and ethnic attributions of meaning pervade all or almost all spheres of life. Under these circumstances ethnic identity is totalizing or summative—it draws in to itself everything else" (Fenton 2003:115).

This kind of approach to the House of Israel have important implications. If we investigate one aspect of their lives we must see how it stands in connection with their world of meaning as a whole. Everything was interconnected, a tapestry of meaning as it were, where eating food according to the laws of *kashrut* was not unrelated to going on pilgrimage, who you marry, harvesting your crops, the way you buried the dead, or the kind of oil you used in your lamps. Think of it as a cultural "ecosystem," where the proper function of one element affects the balance and functioning of the whole.

The Past, Present, and Future

Since symbolic universes are social constructions, it implies they are social products with a history. "If one is to understand their meaning, one has to understand the history of their production" (Berger & Luckmann 1967:98). Israel's symbolic universe was primarily shaped by her relationship with the *land*. The Exodus tells the story of Israelites gaining freedom, making a covenant with God, and entering the promised land. This privilege she lost through the Babylonian exile. Return to the land meant foreign domination, somewhat alleviated because of the Maccabean Revolt, but mighty Rome and her imperial policies thwarted any plans for the covenant promises of the land to take the ideal shape. In the process a myriad of Diaspora communities were also established. The Israelite symbolic universe, in its most idealized form, could only take shape through Israel's obedience, the return of the exiles, and the restoration and ownership of the land. Berger & Luckmann (1967:103) explain further that the

> symbolic universe also orders history. It locates all collective events in a cohesive unity that includes past, present and future. With regard to the past, it establishes a "memory" that is shared by all the individuals socialized within the collectivity. With regard to the future, it establishes a common frame of reference for the projection of individual actions. Thus the symbolic universe links men with their predecessors and their successors in a meaningful totality...All the members of a society can now conceive of themselves

as *belonging* to a meaningful universe, which was there before they were born and will be there after they die. (emphasis original)

The "Order" of the Universe

A symbolic universe is also nomic, or ordering in character. People, objects and things, times and places, belong in their proper place. For example, Israelites had a "map" of times. The pilgrimage festivals marked off certain periods as sacred, being times dedicated to God accompanied by feasting and merry making with fellow Israelites. There was the annual Day of Atonement (*Yom Kippur*), the feast of New Year (*Rosh ha-Shana*), and other festivals such as *Purim* and *Hanukkah*. This was interspersed by the weekly celebration of the Sabbath, the day of rest, but observed by burning candles and attending the local assembly (synagogue) for instruction in the law and the prophets. The yearly calendar was contested by the various Israelite sects—should the lunar or solar calendar be observed? Most Israelites observed the lunar calendar along with the temple, but the Dead Sea Scrolls, *Jubilees*, and *1 Enoch* favor the solar calendar. The question arose: Are the sacred days "below" in sync with those observed "above," where, for example, the angels also observe the Sabbath?

People also had a certain order and hierarchy about them. This facilitates the formation of individual identity, your place being relative to significant others as "equal," "above" or "below" you. This sets out the parameters of legitimate or illegitimate social interaction. "The symbolic universe assigns ranks to various phenomena in a hierarchy of being, defining the range of the social within this hierarchy" (Berger & Luckmann 1967:102). For Israel this hierarchy of being was primarily objectified in the purity order. To be "pure/clean" refers to wholeness or normality, everything that fits into God's perfect order of creation. Impurity could be acquired through transgressing the law, but essentially had to do with the changes of status.

> What is at one and the same time intact and in its place is pure, *tahor*. Conversely, what is impure, *tame*, presupposes mixture and disorder. Hence the attention given to extreme situations, to the margins, to beginnings and ends, to the frontiers of otherness in all its forms ... Thus the margins of the body are dangerous. The skin diseases, bodily secretions, the emissions of sperm and blood, excrement, by blurring the frontiers between the interior and the exterior, threaten physical integrity. (Schmidt 2001:91)

This concern for "hybridity" or "mixity" also extended to other aspects of Israelite life (Schmidt 2001:94). Clothing could not be made of hybrid fabrics, woven from wool and linen, in order to prevent the mixing of animal with vegetable (Lev 19:19; Deut 22:11). The farmer must preserve the perfect order of creation by not mating two different species of his livestock (Lev 19:19), or not yoking together the ox and the donkey (Deut 22:10), or not sowing different seeds together on his agricultural land (Lev 19:19; Deut 22:9).

The purity laws are found mainly in Leviticus 12 (childbirth), Leviticus 13–14 (skin disease), Leviticus 15 (bodily emissions), Numbers 19 (death), and Leviticus 11; Deuteronomy 14 (food). Here are a few examples of what is involved. After childbirth a woman was impure for either forty days (after the birth of a son) or eighty days (after the birth of a daughter). She was not allowed to enter the temple or touch "holy things," that is, tithes or offerings destined for the temple. Menstruation leads to week long state of impurity. Anybody touching a menstruant, her bed or chair was impure for a day (the same length required for purification after contact with semen). Death was the most severe form of "change of status." One contracted corpse impurity through physical contact or by being in the same room. In our period a person even contracted it by "overshadowing" the corpse (by walking over a grave) or by being "overshadowed" by one. Here purification required seven days. Especially the priesthood and the temple had to be protected from contracting corpse impurity. Nothing associated with "death" belongs to the space where God is present. Even the high priest was not allowed to contract corpse impurity when his father or mother died (Lev 21:1–11).

On a social level, however, purity refers to persons, animals and things who properly belong to a society, and can fully engage or be used within that society. It refers to a person or something which is in the correct state at the correct place at the correct time. "Impurity/unclean" is a state which has been likened to "dirt" (Douglas 1966). It is something that is not welcome, something out of place, such as dirt trampled on your carpet from the garden, or a bird following its natural inclinations and leaving the splattered evidence on your recently washed and polished car. You as a person, or the society as a whole, must get rid of the "dirt" or avoid contact with it as far as possible. So the categories of pure and impure in first-century Israel were social constructs, their primary concern being to preserve the wholeness or integrity of society, and its identity

A Socio-Cultural Model of Israelite Ethnicity

and boundaries. They serve to include or exclude. And the wholeness and integrity of a society depended on the wholeness and integrity of individual bodies making up that society (Malina 1993: 149–183; Neyrey 1988; 1996). Neyrey (1996:89) explains:

> The body is a model that can stand for any bounded system. Its boundaries can represent any boundaries that are threatened or precarious . . . Just as the social body is perceived in some way as an ordered, structured system that is concerned to affirm and protect its order and its classifications, so the physical body of individuals in that same society mirrors the social sense of order and structure. Just as the social body is concerned about its boundaries (frontiers, city walls, gates), so too the physical body is the object of concern regarding its surface (skin, hair, clothing) and orifices (eyes, mouth, genitals, anus).

This ordering of society is symbolized by the temple complex's planning and architecture (Schmidt 2001:32–33). Look at the following graphic and see how Israel's symbolic universe was hierarchically structured which of course determined the horizontal dimension of social interaction and involvement in the temple cult. The graphic is a representation of what is pure/clean (top), in it most absolute sense, and therefore fit for communion with God, balanced by what is impure/unclean (bottom),[1] and how this social structure is mirrored in the temple complex's planning:

---

1. Simplified from Malina (1993:160–65).

PURE / CLEAN

(Allowed participation in the temple cult and allowed access to inner courts)

People	Animals (fit for sacrifice or table use)
Priests Levites Israelites ("laymen")	Unblemished clean animals fit for the altar Animals with parted hooves and who chew the cud

Related to the observance of purity laws:

Food prepared according to the laws of *kashrut*

Avoiding contracting impurity where possible (i.e., improper table fellowship, idolatry, "lepers," carcasses, menstruants, etc.

Ritual immersion

Bringing of appropriate "sin" and "guilt" offerings, etc.

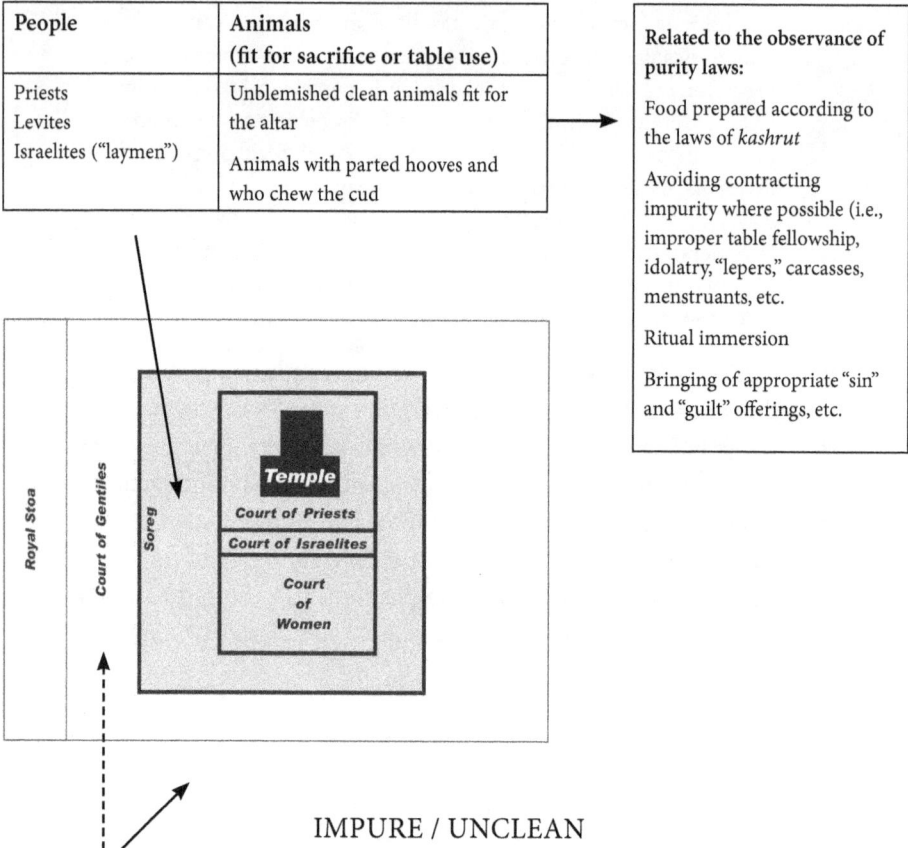

IMPURE / UNCLEAN

(Access to the temple's inner courts or temple complex or Jerusalem not allowed)

People	Animals
Those born with sexual deformities. The blind, cripple, lame, and lepers, etc. Gentiles	Animals who neither have cloven hoofs nor chew the cud (includes predators and carrion eaters) "Swarming and creeping things"

Israelites in a temporary state of impurity

A Socio-Cultural Model of Israelite Ethnicity

So people and places were classified, relating to whom may have access to the temple and its various courts subject to various degrees of purity (cf. *m. Kel.* 1.6–9; *t. Meg.* 2.7). On a larger scale, it determined the permitted levels of social interaction. Within the grey area, that is, beyond the *soreg*,[2] were allowed the priests, Levites and other full-blooded Israelites. This represented the most ideal Israel, those of pure genealogical descent, those who could freely intermarry (but subject to the capacity of having children), and so they can properly transfer their inherited status (through the father) to a new generation. But even here we find a hierarchy, since only priests were allowed to serve in front of the temple around the altar (Court of Priests). Priests with any physical deformity, however, were banned from temple service (Lev 21:17–21). Male Israelites had access only as far as the Court of Israelites, next to where the priests did their work. The access of female Israelites and children did not extend beyond the Court of Women. And whatever your level of access, it had to be done in a state of ritual purity and several immersion pools were located to the south of the temple complex to help with this purpose.

The classification of people is mirrored by the classification of animals, be they for sacrifices/offerings brought to the temple or for consumption at home. Fit for sacrifice at the altar (located in the Court of Priests) were unblemished clean animals with or without a required age or quality (Lev 1:3, 10; 4:3, 23, 28; 5:15, 18; 9:3; 22:20; 23:18; Num 3:13; 8:17–18; 18:15), which also can only come from domestic animals (Lev 1:2). Then follows other unblemished clean animals fit for table use, categorized according to those who properly belong to the land, water, and air (Lev 11; Deut 14:4–6), that is, those perceived not to have any "hybridity" or "mixture" about them.

At the bottom of the scale are those things unclean. On the one hand they are people who can not marry or have sexual relations (eunuchs from birth, those with deformed sexual features, hermaphrodites), and so could not transmit Israelite status or ethnic identity. Gentiles, as were "creeping and swarming things" (Lev 11:41–42)—that is, animals perceived to defy proper classification—were an abomination and regarded as "impure" as well. But life is never that simple where things are simply "pure" or "impure," black or white. What we also find are various shades of

---

2. The *soreg* was a chest-high balustrade, about 1.5 metres high, that separated the Court of Gentiles from the inner courts. Ephesians 2:14 refers to it, where it is explained that Jesus "destroyed the barrier, the dividing wall of hostility."

grey in between. There are those people (and animals) who are classified somewhere between these opposite extremes. Let us call them the "inbetweeners," which in terms of people, refer to those who are of questionable genealogical descent, or lacked the capacity to procreate although not regarded "impure" as such. These include the illegitimate children of priests, proselytes, and freed slaves. Beneath them in the hierarchy of being were the *mamzers* (bastards), the "fatherless," foundlings, and manmade eunuchs. Although of questionable status, they nevertheless formed part of Israel.

It should be mentioned in addition that for Israelites this hierarchy of being was also objectified in the system of the patriarchal family (cf. Guijarro 2001). Israelite society, as was the Mediterranean world in general, was androcentric. The father was the unquestioned authority in the household over wife, children, and slaves. He had to protect the family honor, produce progeny (preferably sons) for the ancestors, continue the family line, instil the correct values and way of life in his children. In a way an Israelite father, or in a more abstract sense, Israelite masculinity, symbolized the epitome of Israelite identity, for Israelite masculinity safeguarded the continuing existence of Israel as an *ethnos*. Also compare the following extract from the Mishnah: "Great is circumcision, for, despite all the commandments which Abraham our father carried out, he was called complete and whole only when he had circumcised himself as it is said, *Walk before me and be perfect* [Gen 17:1]" (*m. Ned.* 3:11). The same passage also states that was it not for circumcision (which also points to the covenant), God would not have created the world (cf. Neusner 1988:412). Thus, a circumcised foreskin was the chief marker of membership in the covenant, a privilege enjoyed only by men. Circumcision was also associated with the notions of procreation and fertility (Philo *QGenesis* 3.48; cf. Gen 17:2–6; *Gen. Rab.* 25.6; 46.4). It is a symbol that God will make Abraham fruitful and multiply. Not being circumcised probably had the connotation of infertility, and the improper functioning of the male organ.[3] Circumcision also makes visible and solidifies kinship bonds between males, forming a "blood brotherhood" of sorts, and also creates

---

3. This also extends to symbolic usage of "uncircumcised hearts" (Jer 9:25; Deut 10:16; Ezek 44:7; Lev 26:41), "ears" (Jer 6:10), and Moses' speech impediment is described as a problem of having "uncircumcised lips" (Exod 6:12, 30). "Uncircumcised hearts, ears, and lips are organs that cannot do what God intended them to do" (Eilberg-Schwartz 1990:149).

intergenerational continuity or patrilineal descent (Eilberg-Schwartz 1990:162, 171). It was a matter of being "the son" of so and so. Therefore Israelite masculinity, having to do with mastery over wife and children, the procreation of "holy seed" and progeny for the ancestors, and being a member of the covenant through circumcision, all these contributed towards the order and content of Israel's symbolic universe.

Protecting Your Universe

Symbolic universes need to be maintained and protected from threats, both from without and from within (cf. Berger & Luckmann 1967:108–14). Even full-blooded Israelites inevitably had to contract impurity due to sexual intercourse, menstruation, childbirth, and contact with a corpse, not to mention transgression of the law. In order to rectify any form of deviance, universe-maintenance employs "therapy": "Therapy entails the application of conceptual machinery to ensure that actual or potential deviants stay within the institutionalized definitions of reality, or, in other words, to prevent the 'inhabitants' of a given universe from 'emigrating' ... This requires a body of knowledge that includes a theory of deviance, a diagnostic apparatus, and a conceptual system for the 'cure of souls'" (Berger & Luckmann 1967:113). If Israelites contracted impurity, this could be remedied by bringing various sacrifices and offerings at the temple, the passing of time, as well as undertaking ritual immersions. Have a look at the following table to see how various states of impurity were addressed:

Impurity	Duration	Remedy	Reference
Corpse impurity	7 Days	Slaughter and burning of red heifer outside temple. Sprinkled with ashes on third and seventh day. Immersion and washing of clothes on seventh day.	Numbers 19

Impurity	Duration	Remedy	Reference
Child birth	40 Days (birth of a son) 80 Days (birth of a daughter)	Ritual immersion and presentation of "burnt" and "sin" offerings	Lev 12:1–8
Mensruation	7 Days	Ritual immersion	Lev 15:19
Midras impurity (contact with menstruant's bed or chair)	Until sunset	Ritual immersion and washing of clothes	Lev 15:19–23
Irregular discharges (from male and female genitalia)	7 Days	Ritual immersion and presentation of "sin" offerings	Lev 15:1–15, 25–30
Nocturnal emission (from a man)	Until sunset	Ritual immersion and washing of everything that came into contact with semen	Lev 15:16–17
Sexual intercourse	Until sunset	Ritual immersion	Lev 15:18
Carcasses and "swarming things"	Until sunset	(Ended at sunset)	Lev 11:29–38
Skin disease	Indefinite / temporary	Inspection by priest and "sin" offerings	Lev 13–14
Transgressing the law: —knowingly	Indefinite / temporary	Presentation of "guilt" offerings (subset of "sin" offerings)	Lev 6:2–7
—unknowingly	Indefinite / temporary	Presentation of "sin" offering	Lev 4:27–35

A Socio-Cultural Model of Israelite Ethnicity

The above table is not exhaustive, but what we recognize here is deviance, diagnosis, and cure. In this manner Israelites could maintain their position within the covenant, or the Israelite symbolic universe, and so the privilege of communion with God and his holy people. That the average Israelite had a general concern for purity is evidenced by the widespread refusal to eat with Gentiles, endogamous marriages, and the existence of immersion pools in territories dominated by an Israelite population. What the *soreg* in the temple complex symbolized—separation between Israelite and Gentile, between clean and unclean—had its ritual counterpart in ritual immersion. In addition to this is the ubiquitous presence of stone vessels in Judea, Galilee, and the Golan in realms of domestic space excavated by archaeologists (cf. Sanders 1992:222–29; Reed 2000:44–51; 1999:95–102). The Mishnah prescribes that vessels made of stone can not contract impurity (*m. Kel.* 10:1). What these practices point to is the communication of *similarity* vis-à-vis co-ethnics (purity/wholeness/belonging) and the communication of *difference* in opposition to ethnic "others." And remember, communicating identity is *doing* something. Ethnic identity is a *social activity*. For Israelites to observe the law was about communicating group identity and membership, about adhering to group values and participating in a shared universe—its was *not* about performing "legalistic works righteousness." But more on this will be said in chapter 3.

The kind of worldview outlined above, centered on the temple and its purity system, would have been mediated to the average Israelite through the local assemblies ("synagogues") through priests (Sanders 1992:170–82; cf. Stegemann & Stegemann 1999:140). The assembly did not function similar to a "church," but was like a local community center having various social, political, legal and financial functions (Shanks 2001:52–53). But on the Sabbath they would serve as the locale for instruction in the law and the prophets by priests (Josephus *Apion* 2.175–78; Philo *Creation* 128; *SpecLaws* 2.62; *Moses* 2.216; Eusebius *Pr. Ev.* 8.7.12–13). According to Sirach priests were the teachers of the Israelite people (Sir 45:17), and according to Josephus, their rulers and judges (*Ant.* 4.304; 14.41; *Apion* 2.165). Their way of life was a "theocracy" (*Apion* 2.184-7). According to Philo the Sabbath instruction was led by a priest or elder (*Hyp* 7.12–13). There is also the Theodotus Inscription found near the temple mount, which refers to an assembly hall and is dated to the first century. It reads in part: "Theodotus son of Vettenus, priest and ruler of the assembly hall

... built the assembly hall ("synagogue") for the reading of the Law and for the teaching of the commandments ..." (cf. Kloppenborg 2006:251–79; Shanks 2001:51). Schmidt (2001:263) argues correctly that already before 70 CE

> the synagogal institution is a bearer of the thinking of the Temple. Far from being a sign of a decline of the Temple, it is one of the principal vehicles of the extension to the whole of [Judean / Israelite] society of the ritual prescriptions expressing the categories of the sacred and the profane, of the pure and the impure, as well as the mode of classification proper to the thinking of the Temple. As such, the synagogal institution appears as a manifestation of the extension—in the strongest sense of the term—of the Sanctuary.

Now we turn our attention to the possible threats from "without." The Israelites throughout their history were always targets of some or other empire, but particularly Hellenism and the consequent Roman presence brought with them a different view of the world—a different way of "knowing"—and cultural challenges of a different order. For example, the gymnasium built in Jerusalem, caused a dilemma for circumcised Israelites who wished to participate. Since participation required nudity, having a circumcised penis was not so ideal. Should they remain loyal to the covenant (Gen 17:10–14), or perform and epispasm (a reconstruction of the male foreskin)? Young Israelites were encouraged: "Share in the Greek style, change your mode of living, and enjoy your youth" (4 *Macc* 8:8). *Jubilees* insists, however, that it is an "eternal error" not to perform the rite of circumcision and in answer to the Greek love of nudity also explain that Adam and Eve covered their genitals (*Jub*. 3:31; 15:33–34).

The presence of alternative worldviews dotted the Palestinian landscape. You would see temples dedicated to Caesar Augustus ("Augusteums") standing in Caesarea on the coast, Sebaste in Samaria, and Omrit in far northern Galilee built by Herod the Great (Overman et al. 2003; cf. Jacobson 2002:22). Although not built in areas governed by Israelites (Josephus, *Ant*. 15.328–30, 363–64; *War* 1.403–7), they were nevertheless within the boundaries of the ancestral land. Herod also introduced games into Jerusalem in honor of Caesar, built theatres and a hippodrome, and Greek music was performed during festivals. Josephus himself says that the theater and amphitheater are things alien to Judean custom (*Ant*. 15.268). There were other foreign intrusions such as aqueducts, the image of the emperor stamped on coins, or the standards of Roman troops when they marched through the landscape or Jerusalem (*War* 2.169–74; *Ant.* 18.55–59). What about a golden eagle—an impure animal to boot—being placed over the entrance to the temple, and those brave enough to take it down being burned alive (*War* 1.651–5; *Ant.* 17.149–67)? What about the emperor being hailed as "son of god" and "savior"? Then of course there was the *Pax Romana*. It is Rome, sanctioned by her gods, who brings "peace," "order," and "civilization" to the inhabited world, not the God of Israel. Intrusion into the symbolic universe of Israel is also evident in the arbitrary appointment of the high priest by the Herodians, ignoring cries for the selection of someone "more lawful and pure" (*Ant.* 17.207–8; *War* 2.7). If we are walking in Israelite sandals, we will discover soon that we are walking with a limp, or at least with a pebble caught underneath our toes. Quite uncomfortable and annoying, but at least we are walking.

It also became a question of which way of life is the superior? When one symbolic universe reacts to another, it employs what Berger & Luckmann refers to as "nihilation," which is to "liquidate conceptually everything outside the same universe ... nihilation denies the reality of whatever phenomena or interpretations of phenomena [that] do not fit into that universe" (Berger & Luckmann 1967:114). Two methods can be employed to achieve this end. First, the phenomena are given a negative ontological status, regarded as inferior, and should not be taken seriously. Second, deviant phenomena are engaged with concepts belonging to your own universe. These mutually complimentary ways of nihilation are evident in Israelite reactions to the threat of acculturation, and should also be seen in relation to the evaluative dimension of group identity and membership discussed in chapter 1. As already mentioned, Israelites fostered a positive self-concept positively stereotyping co-ethnics and negatively stereotyping the "other." Intermarriage was, as an ideal, forbidden. The idolatry and sexual immorality ("lawlessness") of Gentiles was pointed out. The best way to protect your universe is to create social distance where possible, and indeed, where seen as absolutely necessary. At the time of the Maccabean Revolt, the book of Jubilees encouraged the Israelites: "keep the commandments of Abraham, your father. Separate yourself from the gentiles, and do not eat with them ... Because their deeds are defiled, and all their ways are contaminated, and despicable, and abominable" (*Jub.* 22:16). This form of "nihilation" is another example of "boundary talk," of "us" versus "them."[4] Being holy and committed to God, that is, ascribing to the right values and way of seeing the world, had its social counterpart in choosing with whom you eat. The sharing of food and table-fellowship "symbolize social identity and solidarity ... inclusivity or exclusivity" (Elliott 1991:105).

Of course, sometimes Israelites reacted violently. The Maccabean and subsequent revolts can be described as a form of *ethnicism*, "a collective movement, whose activities and efforts are aimed at resisting perceived threats from outside and corrosion within, at renewing a community's forms and traditions, and at reintegrating a community's members and strata which have become dangerously divided by conflicting pressures ... [E]thnicism has manifested three broad aims in antiquity ... territorial restoration, genealogical restoration and cultural renewal" (Smith 1986:50–51). Anthony Smith (1986:55–56) explains further that ethnicism is fundamentally defensive, provoked by military threat, socio-economic challenges, and cultural contact.

The story of *Joseph and Asenath* is another illustration of "nihilation." Asenath's infatuation with Joseph is accompanied by her becoming painfully aware that the gods she worshipped and the food that she ate was completely wrongheaded. As an alternative, she is offered the opportunity to become an Israelite, to partake of the "bread of life," the "cup of immortality" and the "ointment (oil) of incorruption,"[5] which on the surface level refers to Israelite food laws and ritual purity, but on a deeper level is about Israelite identity and way of life (Chestnut 2006:360–61). But generally speaking, outside the Israelite symbolic universe existed

---

4. Food, meals, and table fellowship served as grounds for distinction both from Gentiles, and from other Israelites not deemed to follow acceptable standards of purity (Dan 1:1–16; Jdt 10–12; Add Esth 14:17; *Jub.* 22:16; 1 Macc 1:62–63; 2 Macc 6:18–21; 7:1; *3 Macc* 3:4–7; *Let. Ar.* 128–42; *Sib. Or.* 4:24–30; 1QS 6.2–23; 7:15–20; 8.16–19; 1 QSa 2.11–22; Acts 10:28; 11:2–3; Gal 2:11–12). According to Esler (1998:94–97), Judeans as a general rule refrained from eating with gentiles (cf. Hecataeus of Abdera (322–285 BCE), *Aegyptiaca*, cited in Diodorus Siculus, *Bibliotheca Historica* 40.3.4; Apollonius of Molon (first century BCE), *de Iudaeis*, referred to by Josephus *Apion* 2.148, 258; Diodorus of Siculus (writing 60–30 BCE), *Bibliotheca Historica* 34.1.2; Pompeius Trogus (around turn of era), *Historicae Philippae*, book 36, cited in Justin's *Epitome* 1.15; Tacitus (early second century CE), *Hist.* 5.5.2; Philostratus (writing late second and early third century), *Vita Apollonii* 5.33).

5. The purity of bread, wine and oil is insisted upon in the Temple Scroll (11QTemple 47.5–14) and the Talmud places a ban on Gentile "bread, wine, and oil" (*b. A.Z.* 36a-b; *b. Shab.* 17b).

A Socio-Cultural Model of Israelite Ethnicity

idolatry, contamination, sexual immorality, incorrect "knowledge," bogus values, in short, "lawlessness." So far as Israelites were concerned, the Gentiles for now have all the power, the armies, and the will to crucify, plunder and abuse, but they would say *we* have the correct "knowledge" and understanding of how the world really works. One day *our* view of the world, *our* identity, *our* values, *our* honor, *our* loyalty to our patron, and everything *we* hold to be true, all of this will be vindicated. Maybe some of you Gentiles will be invited to participate. Maybe you will be destroyed.[6] But anyhow, *we* are right—you are wrong. Do you want to know why? For to the Israelites "alone did the great God give wise counsel and faith and excellent understanding" (*Sib. Or.* 3:584–85). *We* are the teacher of the nations, a light to the blind (Rom 2:17–20). Jubilees 15:31 also states that God caused for spirits to rule over the Gentiles to led them astray and it is hoped for Jacob: "May the nations serve you, and all nations bow down before your seed" (*Jub.* 22:11; cf. 26:23).

When Israelites had to oppose an alternative symbolic universe they sometimes used the sword, but mostly turned to their "superior" cultural tradition encoded in their Scriptures and their social memory, the inheritance from their forefathers, to offer grounds for comparison and resistance. They employed what anthropologists call ethno-symbolism, the nostalgic use of the past, in order to endure or adapt to current challenges (Duling 2005:127).

Who "Knows" Best?

The last element of the symbolic universe we will discuss here is its maintenance by "experts." As more complex forms of knowledge appear, "they claim ultimate jurisdiction over that stock of knowledge in its totality." These universal experts "claim to know the ultimate significance of what everybody knows and does" (Berger & Luckmann 1967:117). Now one of the consequences "is a strengthening of traditionalism in the institu-

---

6. There were conflicting views on the participation of Gentiles in the future age. First, there was the view that they can become proselytes in the present (*2 Bar.* 41:1–6; 1 QS 6:13–15; CD 14:4–6), but there is no possibility for conversion or even the presence of Gentiles in the future age (Sir 36:1–9; *Jub.* 24:29f.; *1 En.* 90:19; *Pss. Sol.* 17:24; *Sib. Or.* 3:670–2; *4 Ezra* 8:56–58; CD 4:7–12; *t. Sanh.* 13.2; *b. A.Z.* 3b; *Pesik. Rab.* 161a). Second, the Gentiles will be converted, saved or gather to Zion as a consequence of Israel being saved (*Sib. Or.* 3:616f.; 3:710–20; 3:772–73; *1 En.* 10:21; *T. Sim.* 7:2; *T. Levi* 8:14; *T. Naph.* 8:2–4; *T. Ash.* 7:3; *T. Benj.* 9:2; 11:1–3; *T. Gad* 7:2).

tionalized actions thus legitimated, that is, a strengthening of the inherent tendency of institutionalization toward inertia" (Berger & Luckmann 1967:117). The Israelite parallel is obvious in their system that functioned as a theocracy, where priests perform their sacrificial duties in the temple, receive scribal training, education in the "knowledge" of their universe, the Tanak, and where they function as teachers and judges in the assemblies. They therefore also had a *political* and *judicial* function. They functioned as the "brokers" of God's patronage. At the apex was the high priest, the *ought-to-be* ruler of the people, but acting more as a mediator between them and the Roman authorities and/or their appointed rulers (kings, ethnarchs, tetrarchs). But the priests did not have it all their own way. Other "expert groups" or self-styled "brokers" also appeared, such as the Ḥaverim, Pharisees and Essenes, for example, having their own brand of Israelite "knowledge."

It needs to be emphasized that here we do not have to do with teachers of "religion" as understood in the modern western sense, where various evangelists, pastors, and priests engage in some or other "religious" competition for followers or make claims about "religious truth." Smith (1986:43) makes the important observation that in pre-modern eras, "what we grasp as religious competition may equally well be understood as ethnic competition for the monopoly of symbolic domination and communication in a given population, whose 'ethnic' profile is as much *shaped* by priestly and scribal activities as it is reinforced" (emphasis original). In other words, the various Israelite sects, even some branches of the first Messianists, should be approached in a way that they had particular understandings of what it meant to be an Israelite. Especially the "knowledge" of the Messianists represented by Q and Matthew for example, was about bringing the Israelite symbolic universe to function the way it ought to function as per the social vision of Jesus, who said to his followers: "You who have followed me will sit on thrones judging [= liberating/establishing justice for] the twelve tribes of Israel" (Q 22:28, 30; cf. Horsley 1995:39; Horsley & Draper 1999:69).

A SOCIO-CULTURAL MODEL OF ISRAELITE ETHNICITY

When we combine the above insights with the work of chapter 1, we can propose a socio-cultural model of Israelite ethnicity (see pp. 64–65). It consists of two main parts, a graphic and six statements, each part serv-

A Socio-Cultural Model of Israelite Ethnicity

ing a specific function, yet related to the other, and combining to explain the essential features of Israelite ethnic identity. The six statements on the right—adapted to the needs of Israelite ethnic identity—have already been explained in chapter 1, therefore they need not be treated again here, apart from the necessary modifications that "speak" to the graphic and which will be explained below. The graphic on the left, and our main focus from hereon, takes its inspiration from the work covered in chapter 2, and attempts to function as a pictorial representation of the Israelite symbolic universe. It is a visual representation, a "birds eye view" so to speak, of the Israelite "world" (their "knowledge"), their social construction of reality, how it is legitimated, what it consists of, and how that world is maintained through social and cultural processes.

Our understanding of any subject matter is always subject to change and improvement. The model as a whole is therefore heuristic and must be regarded as a means to an end and not as an end in itself. It is an etic model, we being outsiders, attempting to reconstruct how Israelites, especially those living within ancestral Israel itself, understood their world. It also functions as an aid for us to understand the theoretical social and ethnic processes that lay behind it. As a necessity the overall approach is done to a relatively high degree of abstraction and so oversimplifies the information. It does not take regional differences into account, neither social status nor hierarchy, and since it was a male dominated world it favours the view of male Israelites and so ignores (although we must not discount) the role that gender played in ethnic self-ascription. In other words it must not be assumed that the model presupposes that every Israelite is a "perfect fit," as peasants will give greater concern and attention to certain aspects of their identity when compared to priests or the social elite, and there will be differences between those living in Galilee, the Golan, and Judea, or those living in a *polis* or more rural areas. The model is an approximation, a buffet of choices and possibilities, through which Israelite ethnic identity could be expressed or experienced.

How the two parts of the model interact can most clearly be shown by comparing the graphic with statement no. 4. The two in their own way explain what the Israelite symbolic universe, or its aspects of shared meaning, consist of. Both also explain, however, that the various aspects of meaning or cultural features are grouped, some under the "Sacred Canopy" (= "core values"), and some under the "Habitus/Israel" (= "institutions"), made clear by the following table (on p. 66):

* Patriarchs, Moses, Exodus, Covenant, Promise and Conquest of the Land, Davidic Kingdom, Exile, Maccabean Revolt etc.

** Abraham, Isaac, Jacob, Twelve Patriarchs, Family Ancestors etc.

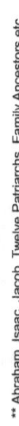

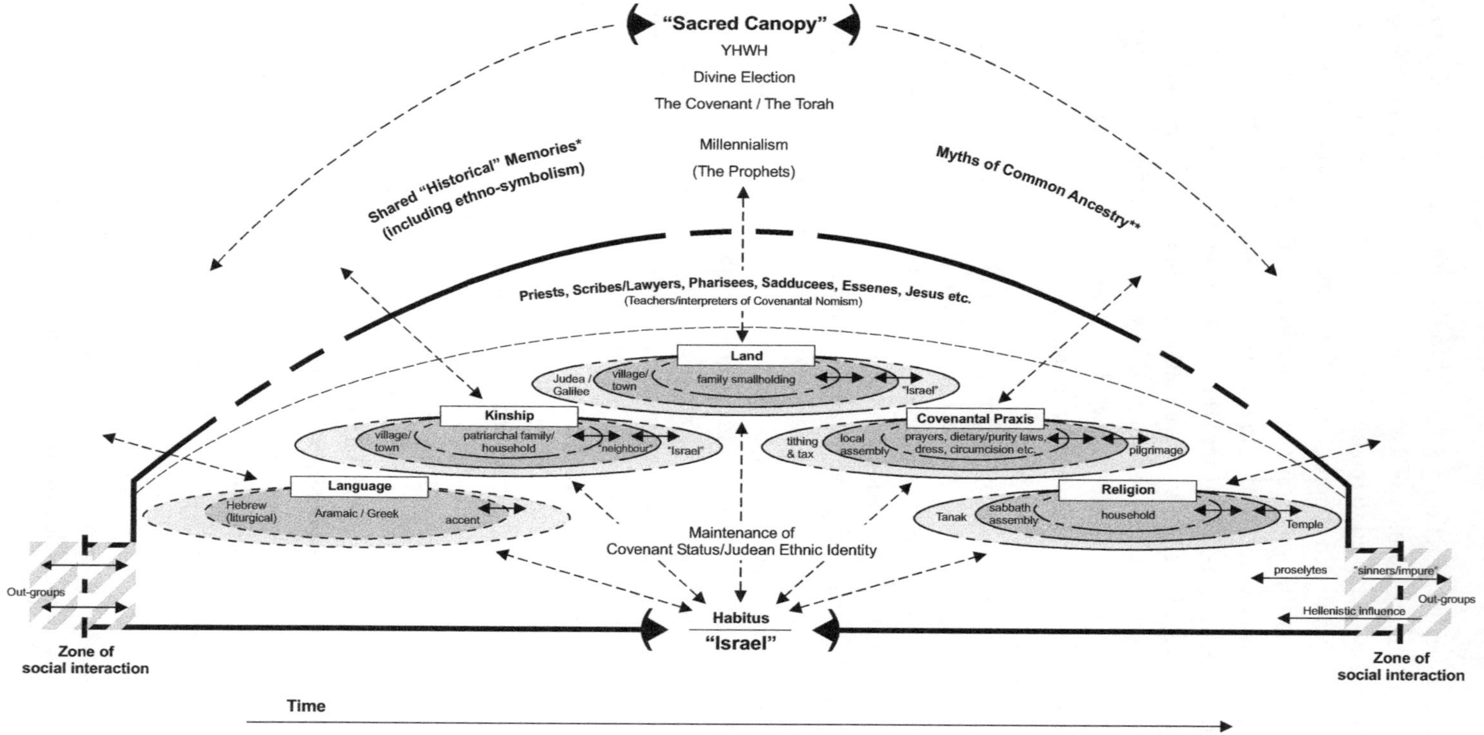

SOCIO-CULTURAL MODEL OF ISRAELITE ETHNICITY

1. *Israelite ethnicity is a form of social identity and relation*, referring to a group of people ("Israel") who ascribe to themselves and/or by others, a sense of belonging and a shared cultural tradition;

2. *Israelite ethnicity is socially (re)constructed*, the outcome of enculturation and socialization, as well as the social interaction with "others" across the ethnic boundary;

3. *Israelite ethnicity is about cultural differentiation*, involving the communication of similarity vis-à-vis co-ethnics (aggregative "we") and the communication of difference in opposition to ethnic others (oppositional "we-they");

4. *Israelite ethnicity is concerned with culture—shared meaning*—which consists of a combination of the following:

   (a) Widely shared values/norms which govern behavior: God (monotheism), divine election, the covenant, Torah, millennialism, shared "historical" memories, and myths of common ancestry.

   (b) Institutions: a corporate name ("Israel"), an actual or symbolic attachment to an ancestral (or idealized) land, a sacred language (Hebrew) and other spoken languages (Aramaic and Greek), kinship patterns, shared customs (covenantal praxis), and a shared religion;

5. *Israelite ethnicity is no more fixed than the culture of which it is a component*, or the situations in which it is produced and reproduced;

6. *Israelite ethnicity is both collective and individual*, externalized in social interaction and internalized in personal self-identification.

Main Cultural Features of the Israelite Symbolic Universe:[7]

Sacred Canopy (= "Core Values")	**Habitus/Israel** (= "Institutions")
YHWH (monotheism)	Name
Divine Election	Language
The Covenant / The Torah	Kinship
Millennialism (& The Prophets)	Land
Shared "Historical" Memories	Covenantal Praxis
Myths of Common Ancestry	Religion

According to Barth (1969), some cultural features function as emblems of ethnic distinctiveness, while others are played down or even ignored. Those cultural features which do function to serve the purpose of ethnic differentiation are broadly speaking of the following two types. Esler (1998:80) explains: "First, there are *overt signals or signs*, features which people deliberately adopt to show identity (for example, dress, language, architecture and lifestyle). Second, there are *basic value orientations*, the norms of morality and excellence used to assess performance" (emphasis original). The second one plays an important role in identity: "Since belonging to an ethnic category implies being a certain kind of person, having that basic identity, it also implies a claim to be judged, and to judge oneself, by those standards that are relevant to that identity" (Barth 1969:14). It is proposed here that the features listed under the "Sacred Canopy" correspond to Barth's *basic value orientations*, while the features listed under the "Habitus/Israel" set out the more *overt signals or signs*. Taking our inspiration from Sanders' notion of covenantal nomism, the former corresponds to "getting in," and the latter to "staying in" the covenant relationship.

That the ingredients of the Israelite symbolic universe, as represented by the model, is more or less on the right track is illustrated by the following passage from Paul. In Romans we find an emic description of what it means to be an Israelite, where Paul speaks of his co-ethnics in the following way:

> my kinsmen according to the flesh, who are Israelites [*name*]. Theirs is the adoption as sons; theirs the divine glory [*YHWH*,

---

7. For a more detailed description of the content of the Israelite symbolic universe, see Cromhout (2007:117–230).

A Socio-Cultural Model of Israelite Ethnicity

> *divine election; kinship*], the *covenants*, the receiving of the *law* [*shared "historical" memories* implied], the service/worship of God [*covenantal praxis; religion*] and the promises [*millennialism*]. Theirs are the fathers [*myths of common ancestry, kinship*], and from whom came the Messiah according to the flesh . . . (Rom 9:4–5)

Basically everything is present, including the value of honor ("glory") and the institution of patronage (of Yahweh). The cultural features not referred to here are *language* and *land*. But in the very least, Paul seems to help in that our peek through the window to view the Israelite world appears to produce some recognisable features. We can begin to walk in Israelite sandals, although the journey has just begun and we will always have to make adjustments as our knowledge and understanding may allow in future.

The Sacred Canopy

At the top of the graphic is a heading called the "Sacred Canopy." The elements present here are those furthest reaches of Israelite self-externalization, the more mythical or intangible aspects of their "world" (cf. Berger 1973:37–44). It is that part of their world under which the Israelite way of life takes shape, and under which the entire Israelite institutional order is integrated into an all-embracing and sacred frame of reference. It corresponds to Sanders and his notion of "getting in" to the covenant relationship. This is how the Israelite symbolic universe was legitimated. They are the "core (ethnic) values" of Israelites. As Pilch & Malina (1993:xiii) explain, the "word 'value' describes some general quality and direction of life that human beings are expected to embody in their behavior. A value is a general, normative orientation of action in a social system." It speaks to having the right kind of attitudes and adhering to rules of behavior or *communicating similarity*, that is, if you as a member of the group want to participate and share in the group's identity. Arguably it is with these core values where we will find the greatest degree of agreement among Israelites, constituting the source of their collective consciousness or a "minimal consensus" (cf. Schmidt 2001:23).

So to reiterate, how did Israelites legitimate their world, and by implication, their ethnic identity? What were their core values? Their answer would be something as follows: "Our God (YHWH), the *one God* of the universe, *elected* us, and gave us his *law*, and established a *covenant* with us. Go look at our *history* and God's dealings with our *ancestors*, in particular Abraham, Isaac, and Jacob. Go look at how he delivered us from slavery through Moses, gave us an ancestral piece of land, restored us to our land after the exile to Babylon, and we anticipate the day we will again live free on our land (=*millennialism*)," or something to that effect. All of these cultural features or values outlined here is an example of a communal *mythomoteur*, or a constitutive political myth of an ethnie (see Smith 1986:61–68; 1994:716). And of course, these values are the result of enculturation and socialization, which brings us to the other main section of the graphic, the "*Habitus/Israel*."

The Habitus/Israel ("Institutions")

The Israelite symbolic universe, hence, their ethnic identity, is the result of enculturation and socialization. It is grounded in the *habitus*, the shared habitual dispositions of Israelite social agents, or in short, "Israel," which shape and are shaped by objective common cultural practices. Here we encounter the role of affect, the powerful influence of familiarity and customariness in social life, and the strong attachments that result from ingrained habits of thought and social practice (cf. Fenton 2003:89–90). It is here where social categorization takes place, where stereotypes are created, where the collectivist person and "sense of self" is formed through the family, the village/town, or through society as a whole. It is also about having a sense of belonging, deriving a sense of worth from your group identity and membership, and sharing in your ethnic group's social activities, origin and history, tradition, values and meaning. It is here where Israelite social agents acquire competence in their culture and acquire a certain perspective on the world. Ethnicity is a form of cognition—it exists in people's heads, yet made visible in social interaction and observable cultural practices.

The Habitus/Israel operates on two main levels. First, it concerns the dialectical interrelationship between the *habitus* and the more tangible institutions or cultural features of Israelite ethnicity, which collectively, is contained within the thick black lines. These cultural features are the more visible signs used for ethnic differentiation, or alternatively, they are "institutions." If values are the focus points for orientation of action, the way that values are realized are through institutions. "Institutions mark the general boundaries within which certain qualities and directions of living must take place" (Pilch & Malina 1993:xv). For our purposes here we can also understand it as the means to maintain Israelite ethnic identity, or "staying in" the covenant relationship by responding to God's divine election and so forth, and living out the expectations of your group.

Second, it concerns the social interaction with "others" across the ethnic boundary. This interaction is located in the areas demarcated as the "zone of social interaction," but it concerns every other aspect of the graphic as well. It is here where boundary interaction or crossing takes place, being the zone of inclusion or exclusion, of various levels of acculturation, adaptation or resistance. But being grounded in the *habitus*, the interrelationships and interaction outlined here produces Israelite ethnic identity, which involves the objectification of cultural practices in the communication of similarity vis-à-vis co-ethnics (aggregative "we") and the communication of difference in opposition to ethnic others (oppositional "we-they").

For a moment let us turn our focus back to the cultural features within the "Habitus/Israel." Ethnicity theory explains that the most widespread of the cultural features are *kinship* relations and *myths of common ancestry*, with some connection with a *homeland* also being prominent. In the model *land* is given a special place since it was a primary feature of Israelite ethnicity. It is also related to the very strong hopes of restoration that Israelites had (i.e. "millennialism"). Land is flanked by *kinship* and *covenantal praxis* (Judean customs), the latter also being inseparable from *religion*. These were also important vehicles for Israelite identity. But overall, the "Habitus/Israel" points to Israelites living on their land, circumcising their sons, eating food according to the laws of *kashrut*, observing purity regulations, going on pilgrimage, their family ties, endogamous marriages, communal solidarity, and attending the Sabbath assembly and so on. It points to the social process of cultural differentiation and orthopraxy, to covenantal nomism objectified in social activity.

In contrast to the "Sacred Canopy," it is within the "Habitus/Israel" where we will encounter diversity in practice and where sectarian squabbles arose. The main points of contention were the proper functioning of the temple, food and purity laws, proper observance of and interpretation of the Torah, the Sabbath, the calendar and related festivals, and marriage (cf. Cohen 1987:127–134; Baumgarten 1997:7–9).

In contrast to the model of Duling (p. 37) the cultural features here are depicted using more solid lines, in line with the approach taken here that Israelites had very strong emotional—"primordial"—attachments to the various aspects of their culture. Whatever changed occurred was rare, due to them living within a high context culture, and also their commitment to the Torah and tradition of the forefathers, the opposition experienced from Gentiles, and the need to protect their collective and family honor. Language, however, is treated differently, as illustrated by the more broken lines. Israelites on their homeland variously spoke Aramaic and Greek, while the use of Hebrew, although the tongue of creation (*Jub.* 12:26), was not that widespread. Due to the presence of so many Israelites across the empire and the predominant use of Greek, language was not an important means of identifying an Israelite as compared to participating in the communal way of life. Here the production of the Septuagint and the Targums are illustrative of this. It will be an interesting study to see how the availability of Israelite "knowledge" in the various languages actually influenced the nature of that "knowledge" and developed symbolic or cultural thinking.

The cultural features within the "Habitus/Israel" are also distinguished by lighter and darker grey areas, which are related to the different perspectives of those involved with the group. These processes of ethnic identity formation can be modelled on three separate though connected levels of abstraction, namely, the micro, median and macro levels. These levels, as proposed by Barth (1994; cf. Esler 2003a:48–49) and briefly discussed below, are adapted to the needs of our model.

The micro-level deals with the processes that affect the ordinary members of the group with focus on individual persons and interpersonal interaction. It has to do with "the management of selves in the complex context of relationships, demands, values and ideas; the resultant experiences of self-value, and the embracements and rejections of symbols and of social fellowships that are formative of the person's consciousness of ethnic identity" (Barth 1994:21). Think here of the important role of the family, or fictive kin groups, in identity formation.

The median level is concerned with entrepreneurship, leadership and rhetoric. Here processes create and mobilize groups, influencing or prescribing people's expression and action on the micro level. Think here of the role of the local assembly, local leaders, and the influence of the local village/town.

A Socio-Cultural Model of Israelite Ethnicity

The macro level concerns itself with "outsiders" with power over the group. It involves state policies (whether legal or ideological) that allocates rights and obligations, which may involve the use of force and the control and manipulation of public information. Think here of the role of the priesthood, and in particular the authority of the high priest and the Roman prefect/procurator or Herodian ruler he was answerable to.

The micro- and median-levels are indicated by the darker grey areas, and the macro-level by the lighter grey areas. These areas broadly correspond to Malina's "person-sustaining groups." By representing the micro- and median-level with the same color, it attempts to show how closely connected these two levels are in Israelite society.

The last feature of the model we will discuss are the "experts" or "brokers" of the Israelite symbolic universe. They are the link between the "Sacred Canopy" and the "Habitus/Israel." These are the priests, and their rivals for influence (Pharisees, Essenes, Jesus and the apostles etc.) who acted as teachers or interpreters of covenantal nomism, and vied for influence on the macro and median levels in particular. Most of these "experts" had as their main task the preservation of the Israelite symbolic universe, in other words, they were the guardians of Israelite ethnic identity, the guardians of what they believed to be the correct "knowledge" and associated behavior. Smith (1994:712) explains that the "close links between organized religion and ethnicity can be seen in the overlap between their respective myths of origin and creation, in the role of sectarian communities, and above all in the personnel and channels of communication in each case. In fact, priests and scribes, their sacred scriptures, rituals and liturgies have often emerged as the primary guardians and conduits of ethnic distinctiveness."

In conclusion, this chapter attempted to bring together various insights which hopefully, will help us to understand first-century Israelites and their "world," that is, to help us walk in Israelite sandals, which for us is restricted to the power of our imagination and the fragmented information at our disposal. Their cultural "eco-system" was as beautiful as it was strange, as perturbing as it was meaningful. But all human beings are socialized into a world which may be familiar and true to them, while at the same time being bizarre to others. Under all the circumstances they faced, Israelites managed to keep their symbolic universe intact, be it in every day reality or in other aspects that were fostered as an ideal, of promised things to come. Sometimes Israelites "emigrated" from their universe and adopted a wholly new one, with its own brand of "knowledge" and values. One of the most famous examples must be the émigré Apostle Paul, to whom we will devote our last chapter.

3

What Advantage Is There in Being a Judean?

A Conversation with the New Perspective on Paul

> *Ethnicity is ... something we are socialized into. Equally important it is something we can grow out of.* (Fenton 2003:88)

As THE TITLE OF this chapter suggests, we will have a particular look at the evaluative dimension of group identity and membership as it pertains to Israelites in view of the New Perspective on Paul. The question that Paul asked in Rom 3:1 is pregnant with meaning. Considering the work done in the previous chapters and the sense of honor and privilege that would have been cultivated by Israelite group membership, imagine you are walking in their sandals being exposed to the following statements by the Apostle Paul (adapted from the NIV)—remember he is a fellow Israelite, and on top of that, belonged to the sect of the Pharisees:

> Therefore no one will be declared righteous in his sight by observing the law; rather, through the law we become conscious of sin. (Rom 3:20)

> All have sinned and fall short of the glory of God. (Rom 3:23)

> Where, then, is boasting? It is excluded. By what law? Of works? No, by the law of faithfulness/loyalty. For we maintain that a man is justified by faithfulness/loyalty apart from observing the law. (Rom 3:27–28)

> Messiah is the end of the law to righteousness for everyone who believes/trusts. (Rom 10:4)

> For there is no difference between Judean and Gentile—the same Lord is Lord of all and richly blesses all who call on him. (Rom 10:12)

Accept him whose faithfulness/loyalty is weak, without passing judgment on doubtful matters. One man's faithfulness allows him to eat everything, but another man, whose faithfulness is weak, eats only vegetables ... One man considers one day more sacred than another; another man considers every day alike. Each one should be fully convinced in his own mind. He who regards one day as special, does so to the Lord. He who eats meat, eats to the Lord, for he gives thanks to God; and he who abstains, does so to the Lord and gives thanks to God ... As one who is in the Lord Jesus, I am fully convinced that no food is unclean in itself. But if anyone regards something as unclean, then for him it is unclean ... All food is clean, but it is wrong for a man to eat anything that causes someone else to stumble. (Rom 14:1–20)

When Peter came to Antioch, I opposed him to his face, because he was clearly in the wrong. Before certain men came from James, he used to eat with the Gentiles. But when they arrived, he began to draw back and separate himself from the Gentiles because he was afraid of those who belonged to the circumcision group. (Gal 2:11–12)

[We Judeans] know that a man is not justified by observing the law, but by the faithfulness/loyalty of Jesus Messiah. So we, too, believed/trusted in Messiah Jesus that we may be justified by the faithfulness/loyalty of Messiah and not by observing the law, because by observing the law no one will be justified. (Gal 2:16)

Therefore know that only those who are of faithfulness/loyalty are sons of Abraham. (Gal 3:7)

There is neither Judean nor Hellene, slave nor free, male nor female, for you are all one in Messiah Jesus. (Gal 3:28)

For in Messiah Jesus neither circumcision nor uncircumcision has any value. (Gal 5:6; cf. 6:15)

Circumcision is nothing and uncircumcision is nothing. (1 Cor 7:19)

But food does not bring us near to God; we are no worse if we do not eat, and no better if we do. (1 Cor 8:8)

To the Judeans I became like a Judean, to win the Judeans. To those under the law I became like one under the law (though I myself am not under the law), so as to win those under the law. To those not

What Advantage Is There in Being a Judean?

having the law I became like one not having the law...so as to win those not having the law. (1 Cor 9:19–21)

But their [the Israelites] minds were made dull, for to this day the same veil remains when the old covenant is read. (2 Cor 3:14; cf. 1 Cor 11:25; 2 Cor 3:6)

For it is we who are the circumcision, we who worship by the Spirit of God. (Phil 3:3)

What kind of Israelite are we dealing with here? If Paul is speaking of "we," what is he saying about "they"? Based on the sample of texts above, has Paul the Pharisee gone mad? For example, for Paul to say that circumcision or uncircumcision is nothing is like an American politician saying that the burning or hoisting of the stars and stripes is nothing. It is like a tribal chief or shaman in Africa saying that whether one venerates the ancestors or not is nothing. And Paul says those of faithfulness/loyalty (including Gentiles) are sons of Abraham. But a shared ancestry invoked various dimensions (the gift of the land, a common culture, a sense of communal solidarity, etc.) of Israelite identity and which afforded them a special status (Esler 2006).[1]

In similar fashion, for Paul to say that all food is clean is undermining the purity laws and priestly tradition. He dismisses God's perfect order of creation where some things in life were seen as inherently taboo. He also challenges the social hierarchy and social requirement of inclusion or exclusion. If we are walking in Israelite sandals we will understand that Paul is dismantling important elements of our cultural "eco-system" piece by piece. Rather than looking at it as a mere "theological" issue, what Paul is doing is challenging our honor, dignity, sense of worth, and identity. What is he doing to our identity, our sense of honor, the inherent value of our *ethnos*, and the customs of our (fore)fathers? Has he no honor, no shame? Where is his sense of loyalty to our people, our values, and our heritage? What is he doing to the beloved of God, ethnic Israel, and our elect status as the covenant people, we who are divinely favored above all the peoples of the earth, we who have the true knowledge of God and true understanding of how the world should work? What is he doing to our social world, our ethnic boundaries, setting Gentiles as our *equals*

---

1. According to the rabbis, proselytes did not become the descendents of Abraham. In prayers they were not allowed to say "O God of our fathers," but rather "God of your fathers" (*m. Bikk.* 1:4).

before God? What kind of messiah is he proclaiming? Is he not destroying our symbolic universe, our "knowledge" (compare with the model on pp. 64–65)?

Strap on those Israelite sandals again: According to Paul, we do have zeal for God, but it is not a commitment based on knowledge; that is, we do not know or we fail to inquire how God's righteousness is bestowed (Rom 10:2; cf. Dunn 1988:587). Preaching a crucified Messiah, he claims, is a *skandalon* for us (1 Cor 1:23). But how can a crucified Galilean bring honor to Israel (cf. John 1:46; 7:41, 52)? Likewise the Torah, our knowledge and a way of life given to us by God, the "foundation of understanding that God had prepared from the creation of the world" (*L.A.B.* 32:7), the embodiment of wisdom (1 Bar 3:36–4:4; Sir 24:23), our source of pride (Josephus *Apion* 2.227–86)—something Paul now proclaims throughout the entire world has become obsolete (cf. Acts 21:21). He says we are slaves to "the elemental spirits of the universe" (*stoicheia tou kosmou*), we are in "bondage" (Gal 4:3, 25). Are we slaves? He says that Moses was a ministry that brought death (2 Cor 3:7). Our way of life is death, we who "will lead all mortals to life" (*Sib. Or.* 3:195)? And every time we attend the Sabbath assembly he suggests we do not have understanding, for our minds are under a veil when the old covenant is read (2 Cor 3:14). *Old* covenant? Is he suggesting we are not too bright?

What Paul is saying is that simply being ourselves, emulating the ways of our (fore)fathers, being loyal to our divine patron, our law, and being an honorable person as we have come to know it, all of these important elements of our identity are of no special significance. We have no right to "boast," that is, no claim to special honor that can be favorably compared with the ethnic groups. He is in the process of creating a new *ethnos*, a fictitious family, so-called children of God, which he claims to be honorable and true, but in fact it is full of "hybridity," "mixity" and disorder. It is "lawless," that is, *not Israelite*. No wonder Paul was beaten so often by our fellow Judeans (2 Cor 11:23–24). He deserves it!

From Paul's perspective, however, God has created a new (dis)order: new maps of persons and times and places, a new honor standard, a new symbolic universe, and a new set of knowledge (cf. Neyrey 1990). But where does that leave traditional Israelite/Judean ethnic identity?

Moving beyond the question of pure "theology," a plausible context for the failure of the gospel among Israelites had to do with the evaluative dimension of having Israelite identity and group membership, this partially being the result of the Gentile mission (the ecclesiological dimension), and partially the result of the Jesus movements preaching a crucified and universal Messiah (the soteriological dimension). Both of these dimensions have important *socio-cultural implications*, where one of these—already implicit in the New Perspective on Paul and its argument about justification—needs to become more apparent: Paul's arguments against the "works of the law," and the consequent equal participation of Gentiles in the gospel, seriously undermined the traditional value attached to Israelite ethnic identity. It was not so much a "theological" issue, but more so a question of Israelite honor. Yes, there were "theological" objections against Paul (and all the Jesus movements), but for Paul to make the kind of claims outlined above meant an Israel, and therefore Israelite identity, neither vindicated nor clothed with divine honor in full view of the nations, as was traditionally expected. Israel expected divine vindication, not a (re)construction of their identity, least of all a devaluation of it. In the process Israelite "knowledge," at least a substantial portion of it, was also presupposed to be without merit or, in the very least, considered outdated.

As mentioned before, a sense of worth is derived from one's group membership. In the collectivist and agonistic context of Paul's world, one was inevitably engaged in a process of comparison with other groups, one's own group always looking the better for it and something also seen to be divinely sanctioned. If God (or the gods) is for us, who can be our equals? The Romans followed similar logic (cf. Carter 2006). Jupiter granted Rome an "empire without end" and the right to "rule the world" (Virgil *Aen.* 1.254–82; 6.851–53). In Tacitus, a Roman general supposedly explained to a German tribe that "all men had to bow to the commands of their betters" and "with the Roman people should rest decisions what to give and what to take away" (*Ann.* 13.51). Israel—like most ancient peoples—shared in this sense of entitlement. According to *Jubilees*, God told to Jacob that "I shall give to your seed all of the land under heaven and they will rule in all nations as they have desired" (*Jub.* 32:19). Elsewhere it is hoped for Jacob: "May the nations serve you, and all nations bow down before your seed" (*Jub.* 22:11; cf. 26:23). Yet according to Luke, Peter, in the presence of Cornelius, came to the following revolutionary insight: the God of Israel shows no partiality (Acts 10:34). Paul came to the same conclusion: in Messiah there is neither Judean nor Hellene. So what advantage, then, is there in being a Judean? Let us explore this evaluative dimension a little further in view of the New Perspective on Paul.

THE NEW PERSPECTIVE ON PAUL

The "New Perspective on Paul" (NPP) has radically transformed the nature of Pauline scholarship over the last three decades or so. This term was coined by Dunn (applicable to the work of E. P. Sanders) in his now-famous Manson Memorial Lecture in 1982, which challenged the traditional reading of what Paul meant by the "works of the law" as well as his view of "Judaism." Since then, the NPP orbit of Pauline interpretation has gained many supporters, most notably N. T. Wright (1997; 2005). But as it now stands, the NPP is not a monolithic viewpoint—different scholars have their own nuances and opinions about the matter. Even Wright has distanced himself from both Sanders and Dunn, although they all appear to be in agreement on the social dimensions of Paul's argument.[2] This chapter will focus on the NPP as developed by Dunn with whom I am in substantial agreement as to the boundary function of the law and its social implications. At the same time I will also argue that Dunn falls short of doing justice to the logic of Paul's overall argument on justification, and we will also refer to other points of disagreement here and there.

To briefly set out the crux of Dunn's argument, Paul's attitude towards the law was not an opposition to a legalistic works-righteousness or an attempt to earn God's favor, but the use of the law as a social barrier. Paul was opposing specific covenant works, or "works of the law," namely circumcision, Sabbath observance, and food laws. The reason was that "*these observances were widely regarded as characteristically and distinctively Jewish.* Writers like Petronius,[3] Plutarch,[4] Tacitus[5] and Juvenal[6]

---

2. According to Sanders the opposing views Paul mentions were not about "doing" versus "faith," "requirements" versus "trust." "The dispute [in Galatians] was about whether or not one had to be Jewish" (Sanders 1983:159).

3. Cf. Petronius, *Satyricon* 102.14; *Fragmenta* 37 on circumcision.

4. Cf. Plutarch, *Quaestiones Conviviales* 4.5; where he has a discussion on why Judeans do not eat pork.

5. Cf. Tacitus (*Hist.* 5.4) on the Sabbath. Tacitus writes on circumcision: "They adopted circumcision to distinguish themselves from other peoples by this difference" (*Hist.* 5.2).

6. Cf. Juvenal (*Sat.* 6.160; 14.98) on abstention from pork and on the Sabbath (*Sat.* 14.96–106).

took it for granted that, in particular, circumcision, abstention from pork, and the Sabbath, were observances which marked out the practitioners as Jews, or as people who were very attracted to Jewish ways" (Dunn 1990:191–92; emphasis original). Dunn (1990:192) continues that "these observances in particular functioned as identity markers, they served to identify their practitioners as Jewish in the eyes of the wider public, they were peculiar rites which marked out the Jews as that particular people ... These identity markers identified Jewishness because they were seen by the Jews themselves as fundamental observances of the covenant. They functioned as badges of covenant membership."

Wright (1997:119–20) here follows a similar sociological approach to justification and the "works of the law" functioning as boundary markers. Justification is about ecclesiology, not so much about soteriology. "Works of the law" do not refer to a proto-Pelagian effort to earn salvation, but "with the question of how you *define the people of God*: are they to be defined by badges of Jewish race, or in some other way?" Although he also points out that we must not play down the soteriological function of Paul's argument, and indeed in a later work suggests that proponents of the NPP have not given enough attention to the matter of God's forgiveness of sinners (Wright 2005:36). In line with Wright's approach here (and others—see below), we will understand Paul's argument about justification as both soteriological and ecclesiological, and we will return to this matter shortly.

For our present purposes we can say that the typical Israelite observances, or the typical Judean customs, were vehicles to *communicate* their ethnic identity. As Dunn explains, for a typical Israelite ("Jew") of the first century CE, "*it would be virtually impossible to conceive of participation in God's covenant* [or read: Israelite ethnic identity—MC], *and so in God's covenant righteousness, apart from these observances, these works of the law*" (1990:193; emphasis original). So what Paul was opposing was something like Sanders's notion of covenantal nomism, understood as God's grace extending only to those who wore those badges that marked out God's people. For Paul "the covenant is no longer to be identified or characterised by such distinctively Jewish observances as circumcision, food laws, and Sabbath. *Covenant* works had become too closely identified as *Jewish* observances, *covenant* righteousness as *national* righteousness" (Dunn 1990:197; emphasis original). There is more to Dunn's NPP, but further rehearsal is not necessary for our purposes here.

The reactions to the NPP have understandably been "theological" in nature. Some have welcomed the NPP, arguing for the many advantages it entails and helping theologians to recognize the problems of the "Old Perspective" (Thompson 2002). Garlington (2005), for example, argues that the NPP is not an attack on Reformed theology and is an attempt to understand Paul within his own context. Others argue, among other things, that the NPP is contrary to good, sound biblical teaching, or that Paul's arguments against "works of the law" refer to meritorious performance or "achievement," "works-righteousness" and "synergism" (Waters 2004; Gathercole 2002; Kim 2001). Byrne (2001) has argued for the "theological poverty" of the new perspective. Commenting specifically on Romans, he says that Paul's teaching about the relationship between communities is grounded in an intense *theo*logical vision—Paul raises the "God" issue, specifically the "theodicy" issue, in Rom 1:16–17. Through the gospel the righteousness of God is being revealed to both Israel and the Gentiles.

Others critically engage with the NPP, accepting the social dimension it brought to light but also stating we must recognize its "weaknesses." For Westerholm (2004) the primary rationale within which Paul operated was that "Jews" and Gentiles are in need of grace, justified as such through faith, not by anything they do, a rationale which should also take pride of place in contemporary situations. Bird (2005; 2007) in a similar fashion suggests we should not lose sight of the law's soteriological function and that "justification" also addresses the barrier of sin between God and humans. Also, there were strands of "merit theology" present in "Second Temple Judaism" because for some salvation, also when placed within an eschatological context, was by obedience ("works"). And in Qumran literature, "works of the law" also refer to ethical deeds, and not merely to "badges" of the community (cf. 1QS 6–7; CD 5:5–6).

This brief review is barely scratching the surface; but overall, the social dimension of Dunn's argument is either understood to be subversive to Reformed/Lutheran theology or is seen as where the NPP spends too much energy. Paul's focus was on more distinct "theological" issues. As will be argued, however, this preference for "theology" or its separation from the social dimensions in Paul's context is a misnomer. In any event, Dunn would deny that the NPP is subversive of the Reformed/Lutheran tradition, and the scope of the debate—far greater than Dunn ever intended—can be gleaned from his response to critique of his work (Dunn 2008:1–97). Needless to say, a fast and furious battle is raging over the heart of Pauline theology and can be followed on "The Paul Page" on the internet hosted by Mark Mattison.

The strongest critique of Dunn—and Sanders: If one has to sink the NPP, one has to sink "reductionist" covenantal nomism—has mainly been driven to defend the traditional understanding of what Paul meant by "works" and what is seen as his opposition to the notion that a person can "earn" his/her salvation through "meritorious works" or "legalistic works-righteousness." The approach taken here, however, and informed by the social sciences and ethnicity theory, will argue the following. Both Paul and the Israel of his day understood God to be working according to the same fundamental relational principles. In both, God, the divine patron, gives grace, and in both, human beings (or God's clients) must respond by obedience ("works") as a demonstration of loyalty. The difference between the two is the nature and extent of the grace given and the nature of the "works" required. Paul offers the followers of Jesus alternative core values ("Sacred Canopy"), and consequently, alternative "institutions" ("Habitus"), and therefore an alternative way of life or praxis in which those values are realized. It relates to *how* God saves and *who* is being saved. Before we look into this in more detail, however, let us have a closer look at Paul's argument against "works (of the law)."

"WORKS (OF THE LAW)"

If we look at the situation that Paul faced in view of his own time and their typical Mediterranean values, and if we remember their world of shared meaning while also appreciating Israel as an ethnic identity, then important things begin to appear on the surface. As an Israelite your group identity encoded divine favor, righteousness and honor, and these positive elements had to be *communicated*. "Righteousness" implied foremost (social) activity or orthopraxy (cf. *Let. Aris.* 151–52). "Unrighteousness" refers to the status as a "sinner," in other words being a social deviant, which embraced both ethical and ritual aspects of life. So communicating "righteousness" presupposes typical collectivist attitudes where behavior had to conform to the norms of the in-group to avoid ostracism and shame. You participate in the social life and rituals of your co-ethnics communicating similarity and belonging, while at the same time you communicate difference in opposition to ethnic "others."

Here one cannot agree with Smiles (2002), who has criticized Dunn's understanding of "zeal" for the law in that he places too much emphasis on "Israel's distinctiveness" and the law's social function as an "identity" and "boundary" marker—that is, to keep Gentiles out. According to Smiles, what Paul primarily opposes was not "separatism," but "activism," the belief that law-observance is constitutive of the covenant. "Separatism was for the sake of obedience [to the Law]; the reverse was never true" (Smiles 2002:298). But attention needs to be drawn to the following: "activism" and "separatism" were two sides of the same coin. Ethnic identity, when communicated, is both *oppositional* in nature (= "separatism") and about sharing in the group's cultural content (= "activism"). This is especially true in circumstances of cultural contact between two groups or cultures, and especially where the one culture is under threat. Since Israel was in various ways threatened or formed ethnic minorities, obedience to the law was as much for the sake of separatism as the reverse was true.

So performing "works (of the law)"[7] is a visible *doing* of covenantal praxis where you as a group-oriented person lived out the expectations of fellow Israelites, participated in Israel's "righteousness," preserved the customs of the (fore)fathers, and preserved the integrity of your ethnic boundaries. Your honor, more so the honor of your kinship group, depended on it. Dunn is partly correct to insist that "works of the law" in Paul's argument refer primarily to those "test cases" of fidelity to Israel's covenant with God. We can say they are "test cases" for communicating their ethnic identity, referring to the more visible aspects of Israelite social interaction. Beneath the surface, of course, lie the more hidden values of the Israelite *ethnos*; and "works (of the law)" can also refer to their entire way of life, as Paul's more generalized approach to "works" in Romans demonstrate.[8]

---

7. "Works of the Law" appears in Gal 2:16; 3:2, 5, 10 & Rom 3:20, 28, and nowhere else in the New Testament or LXX. In Rom 3:27; 4:2, 6; 9:11, 32; 11:6 Paul simply refers to "works" (cf. Watson 2007:128). Otherwise it appears in 4QMMT; 4Q398, frag. 14–17, col. II; 1QS 5.20–21, 23–24 (cf. Dunn 2008:339–45; De Boer 2005).

8. Dunn has unduly been criticized in that he only focusses on the "test cases," but he also points out that when Paul refers to the law he has the entire law in view, all the prescriptions that influence "the Jewish way of life." He complicates this view, however, by also insisting that the law still had a positive function for Paul, that is, when it is "denationalised" and no longer the sole possession and boundary marker of Israel, and so can still be guide for everyday life, especially in its fulfilment of the love command. Paul had a *narrow* and *broad* approach to the law: one will not be justified by doing the works

What Advantage Is There in Being a Judean?

At the same time, doing "works (of the law)" was also about demonstrating loyalty to their divine patron, a typical thing to do for first-century Mediterranean persons. This had nothing to do with meritorious-salvation-seeking "works," for this is working in a false category, namely *religion as understood as a separate and independent sphere of life*, a category that simply did not exist in antiquity. The only "merit" or "earning" you get is not so much salvation—you already are entitled to it, in a sense "have" it[9]—but the recognition of your social standing and honor as an Israelite doing simply what you are expected to do. Doing "works (of the law)" could also develop to become a form of ethnic competition, continuously upping the ante, proving your group (e.g., Pharisees, Essenes) are more "Israelite" than others. Yes, it was seen as "earning" God's favor in this way, but it had to do with the quality of your "Israeliteness," your orthopraxy, not with the paradigm of the quality of your "religion." It was the quality of your "Israeliteness" or your honor by participating in the Judean way of life that inherently established your "righteousness." Living like an Israelite, that is, within the confines of the covenant and requirements of the law, or simply being an Israelite *is being righteous*. But "righteousness" always remained a *group* and not an *individual* status and activity. Israel (or the sect you belonged to) is righteous—not individuals. If we can see that Israelite ethnic identity, when appreciated as a privileged sphere of being and as a group activity, intrinsically required *communication* of that identity, then Paul's argument against "works (of the law)" can be appreciated in a different light.

How must Paul's argument against "works (of the law)" be understood? To paraphrase his statement in Gal 2:16: *no one will be justified by communicating (exclusive, privileged) Israelite ethnic identity*.[10] In other words, no one is justified by being an Israelite per se, by existing standards of honor, or by living the Judean way of life. "Works (of the law)" is a metonym for the Judean way of life, or differently put, a privileged

---

of the law (attacking the social function of the law), yet one will still be judged by the law (where it still reveals God's commandments; e.g., 1 Cor 7:19) (see Dunn 2008:454–66). This tension in Dunn's interpretation is something that still needs to be resolved.

9. God will have mercy on Israel because of the fathers (*L.A.B.* 35:3; 2 Macc 8:15). Israelite self-understanding advanced the notion that they were not liable to condemnation as the Gentiles were (*Pss. Sol.* 3:4–16; 7:1–10; 8:27–40; 13:4–11; WisSol. 11:9–10; 12:22; 16:9–10) (cf. Dunn 2008:219).

10. According to Bird (2007:117), Paul's teaching on justification confronts "ethnocentric nomism."

identity. But God's saving purposes are not restricted to the realm of "Israeliteness," that is, to the Judean way of life to the exclusion of ethnic "others." Israelite identity in and of itself no longer gives you that privileged asset called "righteousness" (Esler 1998:169). It is this Israelite self-understanding that Paul challenges (Rom 2:17–20; 3:21–22; 4:13; 10:4; Gal 2:21; Phil 3:9). Paul, in other words, is questioning Israelite claims of privilege and the positive connotations of belonging to Israel. The Israelite symbolic universe is imploding under the force of his rhetoric and theology. In this respect the NPP developed by Dunn appears to be fundamentally correct.

From the vantage point of ethnicity theory therefore, Paul is *opposing primordialism*, the strong emotional and psychological attachment to an ethnic identity where it is seen as "given," "ineffable," or "sacred." Paul is attempting to counter their world of shared meaning produced by socialization and enculturation. As I argued elsewhere, he used primarily *theological* arguments to counter the primarily *socio-cultural* reality of rigorous attachment to an ethnic identity–he is not opposing a "religious" system, or a decrepit theology consisting of "works" or mere "human religiosity" (cf. Cromhout 2009). We can contrast the two viewpoints by the following:

Traditional View

"works"/ "obedience"	=	"earning merit"	=	"legalistic works-righteousness"	→	(eschatological) salvation

Proposed View

"works (of the law)"/ "obedience"	=	"communicating Israelite identity"	=	"honor"	→	"righteousness" (having a "privileged identity" in the present)

("you belong to the group";
you participate in Israel's way of life
and help to preserve her boundaries)

What Advantage Is There in Being a Judean?

The former, traditional view is *present-future oriented*; the mistake being made is that Israelites were predominantly living in view of the future, forever laboring to build their credits in view of the upcoming judgment. The proposed view is *past-present oriented*. Israelites were oriented towards the past, according to the typical social convention of collectivist and ethnic groups to embody the traditions of their ancestors in the present. The former considers Israel as a "religion," the latter considers Israel as an *ethnos*, an ethnic identity. The former sees Paul as opposing a "theology," the latter as Paul opposing the socio-cultural self-understanding of an *ethnos*. The former looks at achieving (future) salvation, or achieving a status ("righteousness"). The latter looks at breathing in that realm where God's salvation is already operative, that is, maintaining a status ("righteousness"). The former concerns (a lack of) orthodoxy. The latter concerns *orthopraxy*, one of the distinguishing features of collectivist societies. The former concerns individual salvation. The latter concerns group honor (predominantly of the collective, but also that of the individual), where being honorable in the sight of God was one and the same as being honorable in the sight of fellow Israelites. Here it is interesting to note that Paul separates these two dimensions of honor. Paul calls the "myself as seen through the eyes of others" dynamic as merely "pleasing men" (Gal 1:10). What is important is not honor from men, but from God (Rom 2:29).

The irony is the ontological status of the law and its realization in everyday life was not a primary concern for Paul. It *became* an issue he had to deal with as he attempted to create one people out of the many in view of his mission to the Gentiles—to create a new *ethnos* centred on Jesus Messiah. The "law" issue was an annoying *by-product* of his ecclesiastical vision, something imposed on him by others and continuously gnawing at his heals. This is understandable, because if you are walking in Israelite sandals the law was a core value of your symbolic universe and one of the primary points of orientation in everyday life. It was an essential part of your being and identity. Paul therefore opposed the more underlying issue looming large and obscured by his polemic against the law, namely, the issue of Israel as a privileged identity.

That the law was not a primary issue for Paul is demonstrated by his contradictory approach to it. Various reasons have been given by scholars why the law cannot save (cf. Sloan 1991), but this is because Paul gives no uniform "theology" on the law. It was on the periphery of his outlook, not at the core of his worldview. On the one hand, he describes the law as an inferior, temporary, ineffective and malevolent principle belonging to the old age.[11] God sent his Son to "redeem those under law" (Gal 4:5). Paul writes of Moses as the "ministry that brought death" (2 Cor 3:7). The law creates a boundary between Israelites and gentiles. "Messiah is the end of the law," also in its boundary function, in order that righteousness may become the possession of *all* who *believe* (Rom 10:4). Due to human disobedience, no one can fulfil the law, it brought about death, and gives knowledge of sin (Rom 3:9–20; 7:10–12, 14, 22–25; 8:3); it even "increases the trespasses" (Rom 5:20)!

On the other hand the law can be described as holy, righteous and good, and is spiritual (Rom 7:12, 14). Through faith, the law is established (Rom 3:31); the law can be summarized as the following commandment: "Love your neighbour as yourself" (Gal 5:14; Rom 13:8–10) something that is of enduring significance. And to the detriment of any systematic theologian, Paul can say that the "doers of the law will be justified" (Rom 2:13)!

Paul's inconsistent approach to the law should alarm us to the fact that he was addressing more underlying issues, which on the one hand is God addressing the problem of human sinfulness. At the same time, and being the very occasion for Paul's letters where the law is given the greatest attention, the apostle did whatever he could in a given rhetorical situation to oppose the enduring quality of the law because of its function to uphold social boundaries, as well as its function to metonymically encode a privileged way of life and identity. He did so in *response* to the claims of honored Israelite status, the insistence that Gentiles must *also* live within that privileged sphere of "Israeliteness," where God and "righteousness" were seen as virtually guaranteed possessions. Paul's argument against the law was therefore both soteriological and ecclesiological in that Gentiles are *justified as Gentiles* and should therefore be welcomed in the believing community *as Gentiles*. But the law was like a ball attached to a rubber band–the harder Paul attempted to throw it away, the harder it came back.

---

11. Gal 2:19–21; 3:10, 13, 19, 23–24; 4:9; 5:1, 3; 1 Cor 15:56; Phil 3:9; Rom 3:20–21, 28; 6:15; 7:4, 6.

What Advantage Is There in Being a Judean?

PAUL'S ALTERNATIVE SYMBOLIC UNIVERSE

If the sphere of Israelite activity and identity does not justify, then what does? For many the answer is simple: the individual is justified by grace and his/her faith *alone*, something in principle also agreed to by Dunn.[12] But this is where we will go our separate ways because it entirely misses the point of Paul's arguments, which are found consistently, albeit expressed in different ways in his letters, and which can be summarized as follows:

- *Firstly, Paul gives the followers of Jesus alternative core values centered on God's grace and activity of redemption through his Messiah.* Justification is a divine activity, the privilege of God to give through the sacrificial death of his Messiah, who also functions as a model for group behavior (i.e., "faithfulness," "obedience"). Alongside these are other core values such as the gift of the Spirit, the equality of Israelite and Gentile and God's impartiality, a new covenant, love (as demonstrated by God and Jesus), and a spiritual ancestry derived from Abraham. Here Paul addresses the fundamental problem that characterized the relationship between God and man, namely that of human sin. This is a problem remedied by God and Jesus, and has nothing to do with the mantra of individual "faith" *alone*.

- *Second, Paul gives the followers of Jesus alternative "institutions" by which to realize those values.* Justification is the result of living an alternative way of life, an alternative praxis broadly called "faithfulness," in response to God's activity through Jesus. It is to belong to a new and inclusive *ethnos*, to foster reciprocal relationships, to belong to a fictive kinship group not bound to a specific territory. This is the "Israel of God," the "temple of God," or the "body of Messiah." Here Paul addresses group membership and

---

12. "I affirm," Dunn maintains, "as a central point of Christian faith that God's acceptance of any and every person is by his grace alone and through faith alone ... For my own part, even though it is not the language of the Reformed tradition, I have no particular problem in affirming that the doctrine of justification ... is *articulus stantis et cadentis ecclesiae*; I am astonished by and repudiate entirely the charge that 'the new perspective on Paul' constitutes an attack on and denial of that Lutheran fundamental ... It is *not* opposed to the classic Reformed doctrine of justification. It simply observes that a social and ethnic dimension was part of the doctrine from its formulation, was indeed integral to the first recorded exposition and defence of the doctrine—'Jew first but also Greek'" (Dunn 2008:22–23, 36; emphasis original).

identity and its consequent social activity. Paul replaces one form of orthopraxy (or "works") with another, and again, has nothing to do with individual "faith" *alone*.

The first relates to the *how* (soteriology) and the second to the *who* (ecclesiology) of justification, elements which for Paul were neither contradictory nor to be separated. And when compared with the model proposed in chapter 2, both the new values and institutions given by Paul counter those of Israel's symbolic universe. Our focus, however, is on the evaluative dimension of group membership and Paul's arguments against the law–both as a value and as way of life–and what he offers as alternatives.

The "Faithfulness of Jesus"—the "Righteousness of God"

Our investigation will continue with a brief consideration of the proper translation of *pistis*, and there appears not be no satisfactory equivalent in English. Depending on the context, *pistis* has been translated in various ways (assurance; pledge; proof; evidence; loyalty; trust; belief; cf. Hay 1989). When seen within the institution of patronage and clientage, however, the predominant meaning in the New Testament is arguably that of "faithfulness" or "loyalty," typical values of group-oriented people and owed to persons in whom one is embedded (God, the kinship group) (Malina & Neyrey 2008:165–66). Faithfulness incorporates trust, fidelity and obedience, and is the counterpart of the Tanak's *'emunah*. Paul can even speak of God's *pistis* in contrast to Israel's *apistia* (Rom 3:3), clearly demonstrating Paul's thinking moves within the domain of relationships expressed in attitudes, and more importantly, in concrete actions of loyalty.

This approach comports well with the notion that followers of Messiah are "justified by the faith(fullness) *of* Jesus" (cf. Gal 2:16, 20; 3:22; Rom 3:22, 26; Phil 3:9), a translation already tentatively suggested by Turner (1965:111) and forcefully argued by various recent voices (e.g., Hays 2002; Johnson 1982; Hooker 1990:165–86; Wright 2005).[13] Reading *pisteōs Iēsou Christou* and its variants as a subjective genitive, it points

---

13. Although Dunn does not support the subjective genitive reading, he does hint at the possibility that Rom 3:27—4:25 can be seen as referring to both the "faithfulness of Jesus" (3:22, 25) and to the faithfulness of human beings, or to both (Rom 3:28). In these passages it may refer to the participation of believers in Jesus' faith (Dunn 1997:61–81 (esp. 75–76; reprinted in Hays 2002:272–97).

to Messiah's faithfulness or loyalty to his divine patron, being the very means by which God justifies. One cannot entirely agree with De Boer (2005:204–205) that it only refers to Jesus' faithfulness as it came to expression in his death, that is, more to an objective event than the subjective attitude on his part. Certainly Messiah's own faithfulness or loyalty also comes into play and Paul refers to exactly this in 1 Cor 2:16 and Phil 2:5. Paul describes Jesus' faithfulness/loyalty in different ways, as his *obedience*, or his *love*, or his willingness to be *humiliated* (shamed) on the cross. We can accurately encapsulate Paul's argument by saying "that a (wo)man is justified by the *kenosis* of Jesus."

In terms of Jesus' obedience, he, as the new Adam, got it right where the first␣Adam got it wrong: "For as by one man's *disobedience many were made sinners*, so also by one Man's *obedience many will be made righteous*" (Rom 5:19, with vv. 12–18; cf. 1 Cor 15:21–22; Phil 2:8). Where Adam inaugurated the "present evil age" (Gal 1:4) and the situation of human beings enslaved in sin, Jesus inaugurated eschatological humanity, himself being the "firstborn" or "firstfruits" (Rom 8:29; 1 Cor 15:20) of the age in the Spirit. It is about Jesus "who died/gave himself for us/our sins/the ungodly" (1 Thess 5:10; Gal 1:4; 2:21; Rom 5:6, 8; 14:15; 1 Cor 8:11; 15:3) and "the faithfulness of the Son of God who loved me and gave himself for me" (Gal 2:20). To reject Jesus' sacrifice is to reject grace (Rom 3:24; Gal 6:4).

It is about Jesus who humbled himself and became obedient to death (Phil 2:8). It is about Jesus, "our Passover, who was sacrificed for us" (1 Cor 5:7), being justified by his blood (Rom 5:9). *Messiah* has redeemed us (Gal 3:13), *not* individual faith! Most of these statements are simply "slipped" into the text, something taken for granted and presupposed to be common knowledge. From Paul's perspective, therefore, Messiah's faithfulness should be seen as his loyalty or obedience to the divine patron of Israel, his *entire way of life*, including his loving (sacrificial) service on behalf of all human beings. This doctrine, expressed in various forms as outlined here, was arguably with Paul right from the start and central to his convictions, and when addressing the "works of the law" came to particular expression as "the faithfulness/loyalty of Jesus."

Yet for Paul all of this is ultimately God's doing, which brings us to another dimension of Paul's soteriology. Paul ultimately attributes the activity of Jesus to the initiative of God (Rom 3:21–26; 8:3). "God was reconciling the world to himself in Messiah, not counting men's sins against them" (2 Cor 5:19). It is *God*—through Messiah Jesus—*who justifies* (Rom 8:33). In agreement with Martyn (1998:250, 271), justification is the eschatological and world-transforming verdict of God on human beings. It is God who sent his son (Gal 4:4), who gives us the victory over death through our Lord Jesus Messiah (1 Cor 15:57). In Jesus God's promises are "Yes!" (2 Cor 1:20). This God-*through*-Jesus dynamic appears frequently enough (cf. 1 Thess 5:9–10; Gal 2:1; 1 Cor 1:30; 2 Cor 4:6; 5:18–19, 21; Phil 3:9, and see below). Byrne's (2001) insistence on the "theological poverty" of the NPP is a bit harsh, but he is correct to bring attention to the issue that it is *God's* righteousness that is being revealed through the gospel (Rom 1:16–17). The "righteousness of God" appears in Romans repeatedly (e.g., Rom 1:17; 3:5, 21–26; 10:3), and is interpreted here in particular as the "righteousness of God through the *faithfulness of* Jesus . . . God presented him as a sacrifice of atonement, through the faithfulness in his blood" (Rom 3:22, 25). It has to do with God's faithfulness and the fulfilment of his promises to Israel: "first for the Judean . . ." (Rom 1:16; 2:9–10). But side by side with Israel's priority is Paul's argument for the *equality* of Israelite and Gentile: "also for the Hellene" (Rom 1:16; 2:9–10; cf. 11:26–32; cf. Beker 1986:14–16). So God is faithful not only to Israel, but to all peoples. God is a God of the Gentiles also (Rom 3:29–30). In this regard God's giving of the Spirit (Rom 1:16–17; 8:9–11), his forgiveness (Rom 3:25–26), and the story of Abraham (Rom 4; 9–11), and the Davidic kingship of Jesus (Rom 1:3–4; 15:12) is applicable to all people (Byrne 2001; Whitsett 2000). This is the fulfilment of God's promise to Abraham (Gal 3:8, 14; Rom 3:3, 21–22; 1 Cor 1:9; 2 Cor 1:20).

Interconnected with this is Paul's argument for God's *impartiality*, quite a central theme to all of Romans 1–3 (see esp. Rom 2:11; 3:22, 29). God has judged *all* people to be sinners, be they with or without the law. At the same time, God provides exactly the same means of salvation for "*all* who believe" (Rom 3:22; 4:11; 10:4). This theme of "all" is quite consistent throughout Romans (Rom 10:12; 11:32). Thus Israelites and Gentiles are equally liable to judgment and equally accountable, yet both are given the same means and opportunity for salvation. Paul's argument can be summarized as follows: God treats Israelites and Gentiles as equals (Bassler 1984).

One needs to appreciate Paul's contrast between "works (of the law)" and "the faithfulness of Jesus" as God's righteousness yet again: the former is exclusive, and the latter is inclusive. Paul removes justification out of

What Advantage Is There in Being a Judean?

the realm of Israelite activity and identity restricted to a few, and places it within the realm of divine action where "All the peoples will be blessed through you [Abraham]" (Gal 3:8). Justification according to Paul is not a privilege that belongs to a particular *ethnos*, but has proven to be the exclusive prerogative of God and given through his Messiah for the benefit of *all* the *ethnē*.

It is also in this sense that Paul mentions Israelite "boasting" (Gal 6:13–14; 2 Cor 11–12; Rom 2:17, 23; 3:27; 4:2). If Paul consistently argues for the *equality* of Israelite and Gentile and for God's *impartiality*, as we have already seen, then "boasting" must be seen as something that upsets this status quo. According to Moxnes (1996:24), boasting "was often seen as a demand for public recognition of honor," and Paul rejects any special claims of Israelite identity and status based on their lineage. This view falls in line with Dunn (2008:9, 129 et al.), for whom "boasting" refers to Israelite claims of chosen and privileged status, confidence in their identity and being members of the covenant people. Jewett also points out that "boasting" should be understood within the parameters of the ancient honor discourse. In Romans "Paul's claim is that *all* fall short of the transcendent standard of honor" (Jewett 2003:560; emphasis original). To be "set right" by God's grace (Rom 4:24) is to have such transcended honor and glory restored. As Paul expresses in Rom 3:27: "Where is boasting then? It is excluded!" Believers are encouraged to "boast" (*kauchōmetha*) "in hope of the glory of God" and "in our afflictions" (Rom 5:2, 3), which entails a new form of boasting contrary to the mainstream honor discourse of the first century (Jewett 2003:562). Alternatively believers are called upon to "boast in the Lord" based on God's gift of redemption through Jesus (1 Cor 1:30–31).

The alternative value system that Paul proposes can be summarized as follows: There is no one who is righteous. All are sinners, no matter what traditional identity you may have.[14] Yet, we "are justified freely by [God's] grace through the redemption that came by Messiah Jesus" (Rom 3:24). Paul places Israelites in the superordinate category of sinful human beings, thanks to their common ancestor called Adam. The playing field is made level. So what advantage, then, is there in being a Judean? In this context *none*, because *God* decided who are sinners (i.e., "all") and *God*

---

14. For Paul's separation of "righteousness" from Israelite identity see Rom 3:21–22; 4:13; 10:4; Gal 2:21; Phil 3:9.

acted—through Jesus—to justify those sinners. The Jesus followers are the "holy ones," the ones "washed . . . sanctified . . . justified" (1 Cor 6:11).

Justified by Faith Alone?

If followers of Jesus are justified freely by God's grace through Messiah Jesus, is there anything left to do? Are "works" required or not? The restraints of "orthodoxy" insists the answer is "no." For example, Waters (2004:177), being but one voice among many, states with resolution that "Paul is categorically excluding works as having any legitimate role in justification." Opponents of the NPP also accuse it of being guilty of "synergism," exactly the problem that Paul allegedly opposed. Dunn (2008:71–95) pointed out that Paul's gospel still requires obedience, and that believers participate in a process of transformation in view of the judgment ("final justification"). Dunn, however, says he does *not* want to argue that Paul was synergistic, just that some of the language he uses appears to be vulnerable to the same charge.

Less reserved is Watson (2007:213; see also Bird 2007:155–78; Garlington 2005), who suggests that for Paul, final judgment will be according to "works" (Rom 14:10–12; 1 Cor 4:3–5; 2 Cor 5:10; Gal 6:5), but the "works" he has in mind are those within the context of the "Christian" confession. What then about Paul's arguments *against* "works"? Watson (2007:123–124, 128, 148) who distances himself from Dunn and the NPP argues that "faith" refers to life as a "Christian," the adoption of a new way of life, with its own beliefs and practices, whereas "works (of the law)" refers to life as an observant "Jew"[15] (not merely to some distinctive "Jewish" observances per se). These terms stand for modes of communal life that need to be kept separate. In commenting on Rom 3:21–31, Watson suggests that Paul's contrast between "faith" and "works" (Rom 3:20–22; 27–28; 4:2) does not relate to moral activity or achievement.[16] "Works"

---

15. Cf. Martyn (1998:261), "Works" refer to the "grand and complex activity of the Jew." In contrast to this is Waters (2004:158–70) who argues that "works" in some passages (Rom 11:5–6; 4:4–5; 9:30–32; 10:5; Phil 3:2–11) cannot be restricted to or even refer to matters of ethnic status, but rather refers to human activity, striving and effort. The problem with this is that in the texts cited Paul always is referring to or speaking to Israel(ites), and so is not applicable to general human activity.

16. According to Watson, the "achievement" (and source of "boasting") Paul has in view Rom 3:27–28 refers to the "Roman Jewish Christians as 'boasting' in their law observance, as other Jews do, regarding it as inherently praiseworthy and as a mark of superiority over Gentiles, Christian or otherwise" (2007:251). Paul asks them to abandon

refer to the "Jewish" way of life, as opposed to "faith" that stands for entire way of life for a follower of Jesus. Salvation by "faith" is something found within the Pauline congregations. It is an alternative way of life and social conduct, and righteousness is something attained by an identity based on *faith*, a summary term for the communal and individual form of life created by and oriented towards Jesus Christ (Watson 2007:212, 233).

In the essential details it is agreed with Watson that Paul has in view two opposing ways of communal living, although *pistis* is understood here as primarily referring to "faithfulness" or "loyalty." This term that Paul derived from Hab 2:4 encodes an alternative mode of being now inaugurated by Jesus (Gal 3:25). "Faithfulness" is to belong to the fellowship of God centered on Jesus Messiah, and it is a fellowship not reduced to the mental activity of assent or trust, but the emphasis is more on the activity of the mouth, hands, and feet. Conversion in Paul's world was not measured so much by emotional and introspective experiences, but more so by actions of loyalty/disloyalty to a patron, whether divine or human (Crook 2004). In other words, it requires "works," and in agreement with Thompson (2002:7, 17, 19–20; cf. Bird 2007:178), what James calls "works" (Jas 2:14–16) Paul calls "fruit of the Spirit" (Gal 5:22ff.) and the gospel calls us to follow Christ's example (Phil 2:5; Rom 13:14; 15:2f.; cf. 1 Cor 11:1; 1 Pet 2:21). The charge of "synergism" is therefore from a social-scientific perspective ethnocentric and anachronistic, because theologians do not have an appreciation of Paul and his social world on *their* terms, *their* values, *their* institutions.

The institution of patronage and clientage has already been explained, but for first century Mediterranean persons the value of faithfulness or loyalty to a divine patron, and its consequent realization in "works," was axiomatic and accepted as a fundamental reality. It simply would not have made sense in Paul's world to replace orthopraxy with orthodoxy, "synergism" with "monergism." In his world God was experienced within the context of social relationships, that is, by participating in a community. Indeed, their "theology" would be closer to what we call "sociology." Your relationship to God was about having the right identity determined by the group you belonged to and sharing in that group's values and social praxis. Collectivism *required* the communication of similarity and belonging by *doing* something. What Paul offered was alternative content for that *doing*,

their "boasting," their claim to superiority, and so will facilitate their ideological separation from the majority "Jewish" community.

an alternative *orthopraxy* he labels "faithfulness," being an alternative form of relating to others and being the very means by which his communities related to God. Justification was a *group*, not an *individual* experience. Paul in various ways equates the faithfulness/loyalty of Abraham, or of Jesus or his followers with obedience or with righteousness (Rom 1:5, 17; 4:5, 9, 13; 5:18–19; 6:16; 9:30; Phil 3:9), as opposed to the righteousness Israelites associated with their identity and praxis based on the law.

That "faithfulness" is an expression for a particular way of life is further demonstrated by what Paul writes in Rom 14:1—15:13. Here he contrasts those whose *pistis* is either "weak" or "strong." The "weak" in faithfulness continue to observe the law ("do not eat/eat vegetables," "observe days" etc.), and Paul pleads they need to be accommodated by the "strong." In other words, those who demonstrate an inclusive lifestyle in Messiah Jesus must accept those who exhibit a potentially boundary-creating lifestyle. For Paul the gospel was about breaking down social barriers, not maintaining them.

Alternatively, it is about faithfulness, "expressing itself through love" (Gal 5:6). It is about offering your body as a living sacrifice to God (Rom 12:1). It is to share in Abraham's faithfulness (Rom 4:12, 16). It is also to emulate Jesus's own faithfulness, in other words, his way of relating to God and others (Rom 15:3; Phil 2:5). It is to "put on the Messiah Jesus" (Rom 13:14). Paul writes: "We have the mind/attitude of Messiah" (1 Cor 2:16; cf. 11:1). It is about living according to the Spirit, and not according to the flesh (Rom 8:13; Gal 5:21; 6:8).

Demonstrating loyalty to the divine patron, trusting in God or Jesus, and doing "good works" was therefore one of a piece. Interpreting Paul from a social-scientific perspective reveals that Paul and his congregations would not have suffered from a paranoia over "(good) works," but having a gracious patron, or rather an affectionate benefactor, which the God of Israel has proven to be, meant being a thankful and loyal client, a loyalty that was also expressed by *doing* something. "For we must all appear before the judgment seat of Messiah, that each one may receive what is due him for the things done while in the body, whether good or bad" (2 Cor 5:10; cf. 1 Cor 3:13; 2 Cor 9:8).[17]

---

17. One must also wonder how this paranoia over "works" can be harmonised with Matthew's Jesus, who makes "works" the explicit condition for entering the kingdom of God (Matt 25:14–45).

What Advantage Is There in Being a Judean?

Faithfulness is also about that visible demonstration of participating in the community's life by undergoing immersion (baptism). To relegate this to a potential "work" that attempts to earn salvation would have been a strange notion in Paul's world. Apart from participating in the life of the community, undergoing immersion is to participate in the divine patron's economy of grace. It is the ritual by which a person is incorporated into Messiah, into both the benefits and lifestyle of his faithfulness,[18] into his death and resurrection, or into the life of the Spirit (Rom 6:3; Gal 3:27). It is the means to "put on Messiah" (Gal 3:26-28; Rom 13:14; cf. Col 3:9-10; Eph 4:22-24).[19] Those in Messiah are a new creation and obtain a new identity, as Jesus himself transcends all existing human identities and who is no longer to be known according to the "flesh" (2 Cor 5:16-17; Gal 6:15). So the initiatory rite of immersion included the dimension of entering a new group, "being in Messiah," which at the same time involved the breaking down of social barriers (MacDonald 1999:240). In agreement with Watson (2007), Paul is busy creating a distinct identity for his congregations.

Esler (1996; 1998:215-34; 2003a; 2003c:55) points out that Gal 5:13—6:10 and Rom 12:1—15:3 also deal with identity, in particular the values and quality of the identity that must be associated with followers of Jesus. Paul sets out norms or "identity descriptors" for the maintenance and enhancement of their identity. The Sprit-conditioned life within the community is based on love as opposed to the world outside which Paul stigmatizes as belonging to the realm of the "flesh." Believers must conduct themselves in a way appropriate for family members and not engage in honor contests. Taylor (2005), in a similar fashion, points out that in Rom 12:1—13:10 Paul uses "sibling language." Taking into consideration that the sibling relationship was a central feature in antiquity, and entailed

---

18. Here is where I disagree with Watson, who argues that we cannot speak of the "faithfulness of Jesus," it only refers to the faith (or trust) of the believer. For Watson (2007:231-45) the Achilles' heel of the subjective genitive reading is the verb *pisteuein* (v. 22). The verb according to him does not refer to the faithfulness of Christ, and overall there is no justification for a semantic distinction between *pistis* and *pisteuein* ("faithfulness" versus "believe/trust"). It also does not mean that the "faith of Christ" passages refers to "faith *in* Christ," but the *pistis Christou* phraseology "in itself refers simply to the faith that pertains to Christ, without further specifying the nature of that pertinence," or is connected "non-specifically to Christ" (2007:244).

19. Cf. Martyn (1998:259): "Christ's faith constitutes the space in which the one crucified with Christ can live and does live."

reciprocity among family members, Paul adopted this powerful frame of reference to guide behavior. As a new *ethnos* or family of brothers and sisters, as children of God, believers must look out for the interests of others and engage in mutual edification (Phil 2:4–5; Rom 15:12; 1 Cor 8:1; 14:26). The dominating factor in Paul's thinking is the unity of the community, social integration and mutual acceptance socially enacted by the Lord's Supper (1 Cor 8:7–13; 10:14–32; 11:17–34), another visible communication of faithfulness.

To reiterate, Paul did not oppose a "religion" where Israelite obedience (whether seen in an eschatological context or not) is an inferior theology of humans attempting-to-earn-salvation-by-*works*,[20] rather, he addressed the self-understanding of an *ethnos*. Meaning what? If you take seriously the notion that Israelites, as well as Gentile authors understood Israel as an *ethnos* (cf. Mason 2009:141–84), for our purposes here, an ethnic identity, then Paul addressed the inherent claims attached to *doing anything to communicate (exclusive, privileged) Israelite identity, that God's saving purposes and the status of righteousness were restricted to the realm of "Israeliteness" (works of the law)*.[21] We can contrast the two views as follows:

The Israelite/Judean Way of Life

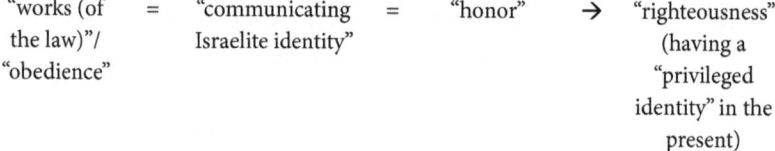

"works (of the law)"/ "obedience" = "communicating Israelite identity" = "honor" → "righteousness" (having a "privileged identity" in the present)

("you belong to the group";
you participate in Israel's way of life
and help to preserve her boundaries)

---

20. Here it is also illuminating what Paul says on "works (of the law)." The problem does not lie with doing "works" in itself, but the incapacity to do those "works." Paul states that "the doers of the law will be justified" (Rom 2:13). Watson (2007:202, 206) also argues that in Romans 2 Paul is not opposing an Israelite "Pelagian" view that we are saved by our own moral strivings and attainments. He is actually attacking the Israelite insistence that their salvation is by grace, based on salvation-historical privileges. It is actually Paul who insists that "works" are the condition for justification. Nevertheless, Paul denies any soteriological advantage for Israel, for God "takes account only of people's deeds, not of their ethnicity–in opposition to the view... that the mere fact of being a Jew is a guarantee of salvation, irrespective of conduct" (Watson 2007:200).

21. This is the view that Paul addresses in Rom 2:14–29.

What Advantage Is There in Being a Judean?

A Life in Messiah

| "faithfulness"/ "obedience" | = | "communicating identity in Messiah" | = | "honor" | → | "righteousness" ("being justified") |

("you belong to the group";
you participate in the life of God's
new and inclusive *ethnos*)

Both of these concern group identity *in the present* where the law and "faithfulness" are held as alternative values and ways of life, or as alternative means of participating in righteousness.[22] Paul's alternative "institutions" can be summarized as follows: "Be devoted to one another in brotherly love. Honor one another above yourselves" (Rom 12:10). So what advantage, then, is there in being a Judean? In this context also *none*, for God—through Jesus—established an inclusive *ethnos* (fictive kinship group) with an inclusive and mutually empowering social praxis. In short, it is to have a new identity "in Messiah."

THE LAST STRAW

Above the attempt was made to illustrate that Paul's understanding of the gospel seriously undermined the traditional value that attached itself to Israelite ethnic identity. In the process he questioned Israelite "knowledge" and the interconnected value system and way of life, and offers alternative "knowledge" ("my gospel"; Rom 2:16; 16:25), that is, an alternative value system and an alternative way of life and identity characterized as "faithfulness" or "loyalty." That this is not merely a figment of our imagination is demonstrated by what Paul has to say about *his own* Israelite identity at times. Here the investigation of Duling of two Pauline passages (2 Cor 11:22; Phil 3:5–6) is very helpful, and we will give a brief overview of his investigations here.

In his study of 2 Cor 11:22, Duling (2008b) combines both the historical and rhetorical critical approaches and understands it as part of the

---

22. This by no means denies that both identities had a future element to them, but the future parousia and/or judgment concerned the vindication of present status, in other words, present group membership and its consequent way of life or orthopraxy. Of course, for Israel it also meant the restoration and ownership of their ancestral land, and on a more comprehensive level, the restoration of their entire way of life as an *ethnos*.

"tearful letter" (2 Corinthians 10–13). Paul's statement about his ethnicity is his self-defense against the "super-apostles" who challenge his authority at Corinth. This occurred at the time when the conflict with them had already developed and reached a climax. Chapters 10–13 articulate carefully formulated rhetorical responses to defend his honor, using irony, self-praise (boasting), and comparison as rhetorical strategies in his defense. It is worth having the passage before us, starting with v. 21b:

> 21b: What anyone else dares to boast about—I am speaking as a fool—I also dare to boast about.
>
> 22a: Are they *Hebrews*? So am I.
>
> 22b: Are they *Israelites*? So am I.
>
> 22c: Are they *Abraham's seed*? So am I.

Duling explains that in his ethnic self-defense Paul is claiming *equivalence*. Being a Hebrew, Israelite, and Abraham's descendent, he is *like* the super-apostles, those very same ones who "boast" in their ethnic identity. It occurs within the context of his Fool's Speech which makes the rhetoric ironic. But the real irony, so Duling explains, is that Paul did not ultimately place any stock in his self-praise. For Paul there was a new *genos* from Abraham, a body of believers "in Christ," and he thought of himself as a leader of another *ethnos*—a metaphorical ethnicity–with different values and symbols. Although his ethnic stock was as good as that of his opponents, there was nothing to be gained by it (2 Cor 12:1).

This brings us to the second article of Duling (2008a), which investigates Phil 3:5–6. In Phil 3:7–8 Paul writes: "Whatever gain/advantage I had I now consider loss for the sake of Messiah. Indeed, I consider everything a loss compared to the surpassing greatness of knowing Messiah Jesus my Lord, for whose sake I have lost all things. I consider them rubbish, that I may gain Messiah" (adapted from NIV). Paul is here specifically referring to what he writes in vv. 5–6, where he is speaking of himself as someone who can also have confidence "in the flesh," even more so than others who put value in their Israelite ethnic identity (vv. 3–4). How can Paul have confidence "in the flesh"? Verses 5–6 we can break into two columns of ascribed and acquired honor:

What Advantage Is There in Being a Judean?

Ascribed honor:
5a: *circumcised* the eighth day,
5b: of the *people/ancestry* of *Israel*,
5c: of the *tribe* of *Benjamin*,
5d: a *Hebrew* of the *Hebrews*;

Acquired honor:
5e: concerning the *law*, a *Pharisee*;
6a: concerning *zeal*, persecuting the *ekklēsia*;
6b: concerning the *righteousness* that is in the law, blameless.

The left-hand column refers to Paul's inherited status, and the right-hand column refers to honor acquired through his training or education (as a Pharisee), his accomplishments (persecuting the *ekklēsia* and his "righteousness"), and his voluntary association (Pharisee) (cf. Duling 2008a:809). Paul can also "boast," since his Israelite honor was among the best of the best. All of this Paul can refer to as "rubbish." So much for having Israelite honor! Whatever force you want to put to the noun *skubala*, Paul relegated to nothing something his co-ethnics would find "ineffable" and "sacred," namely, their identity. He questions their "righteousness" based on their way of life grounded in the law (Phil 3:9). When compared to his new way of life in Messiah, he no longer regards his traditional ethnicity as "gain" or "advantage." This is his virulent warning to the Philippians against those Israelites who insisted on circumcision and whom he unceremoniously refers to as "dogs" (an unclean animal and used in reference to Gentiles; e.g., Matt 15:26) and as mutilators of the flesh (Phil 3:2–3)! Believers on the other hand "are the circumcision, who worship God in the Spirit, boast in Messiah Jesus, and have no confidence in the flesh" (Phil 3:3). In terms of the evaluative dimension of group membership and belonging: How would you, if you are walking in Israelite sandals, respond to such claims?

PERHAPS A LITTLE TOO LATE?

Above we saw that Paul consistently argued for equality between Israelite and Gentile, be they sinners outside of the community, or as a fellowship of believers within the community. Paul in his letters is also like a proverbial bull in a china shop, forever shattering or undermining the honor, integrity, and group boundaries of the Israelite *ethnos*, whether they are followers of Jesus or not. He does all this despite his endeavors to keep his mostly Gentile communities in fellowship with the Jerusalem community and with Israelite followers of Jesus in general. He is also forever playing the comparison game. Life in Messiah, embodying a new and inclusive value system and way of life, a new *ethnos*, is now the exclusive realm of God's salvation. Life as an Israelite without Messiah, or even life as a law-observant Israelite with Messiah has no advantage to it vis-à-vis being a Gentile. This is paradoxical, of course, because Paul is preaching to the Gentiles *Israel's* God and *Israel's* messiah, the promise made to *Israel's* patriarch Abraham, and *Israel's* understanding of salvation history beginning with disobedient Adam. Surely traditional Israel must have *some* advantage?

Yes there is, and the only place where it is explicit is in Paul's letter to the Romans. It can at first be mentioned that In Romans Paul allows Israelite followers of Jesus to be Israelites, but he does so with some qualifications. Evidently Paul is addressing a mixed audience of Israelites and Gentiles, encouraging them to become a united community in an attempt to restore what appears to be a strained relationship between the two groups (Duling 2010; Miller 2001; Beker 1986:11–12). According to Esler, in an attempt to reduce ethnic tension and conflict between Judean and non-Judean believers, Paul wants all persons concerned to internalize that they belong to a new group in Christ. Through their faith in Christ they have been recategorized and now have a common ingroup (or superordinate) identity. Yet, this "includes the recognition that an attempt at recategorization ... is more likely to succeed if its proponent acknowledges the continued existence of the identities of the subgroups and modulates the message to attend to their distinctive outlooks and interests. Much of Romans 1–11 can be seen as taken up with these issues" (Esler 2003c:54; cf. 2003a).[23]

So in Romans Paul wants to accommodate Israelite identity in line with what he says elsewhere (1 Cor 9:19–21). In terms of food/purity laws, if you are walking in Israelite sandals and need to make a distinction between clean and unclean, you may do so. You may also observe

---

23. In this regard Esler (2003c:55) also argues the following: "Rather than positing some sharp distinction between between 'theology' or 'doctrine' (in Romans 1–11) and 'ethics' or 'paraenesis' in Romans 12:1—15:13, we may treat Romans 1–11 as setting out Paul's view of the foundations, nature, and goals of the (recategorized as Christ-believing) group of Judeans and non-Judeans in Rome he is addressing, while Romans 12:1—15:13 covers the norms necessary for the maintenance and enhancement of the identity of that group." Miller also argues that Romans 1–11 is not a theological treatise detached and unrelated to the exhortations found at the end of the letter. "Rather, chs. 1–11 lays the theological groundwork for the exhortations that embody the actual lifestyle changes Paul wants his auditors to embrace in their relations with one another" (Miller 2001:338).

What Advantage Is There in Being a Judean?

special days if you so wish (Rom 14:1—15:11). Paul's overall instruction is that whether people eat, or not eat, observe days or regard all days as the same, this is all acceptable as long it is done for the honor of Messiah (Rom 14:5–9; cf. Gal 4:10). Underlying this is Paul's rationale for Israelites and Gentiles participating in God's new family as equals united by their love for one another. Paul actually encourages the believers: "Receive one another, then, just as Messiah received you, in order to bring praise to God" (Rom 15:7). This is followed by the theme of Israelites and Gentiles praising God together in 15:9–12 (citing several passages from the LXX: Pss 17:50; 116:1; Deut 32:43; and Isa 11:10). Esler (2003b; 2003c) states that Paul's approach in Romans was probably due to negative reactions to his work in Galatia, where he was far less sensitive to Judean identity than in Romans and he came to realize that he should not seek to erase the subgroup identities of Judeans and non-Judeans.

It appears therefore that being an Israelite, but qualified by your loyalty to Messiah Jesus, you are entitled to some dignity after all! Or are you? If we are walking in Israelite sandals Paul appears to give with the one hand and take away with the other. Paul refers to us as the "weak." He even states: "I am fully convinced that no food is unclean in itself ... All food is clean ..." (Rom 14:14, 20; cf. 1 Cor 8:7; 10:25). He also has the nerve to label traditional covenantal praxis such as food laws and Sabbath observance as "doubtful things" (Rom 14:1)! Barclay (1996:212) brings to attention the difficulties in Paul's instructions in Romans. In agreement with Boyarin's (1994) view, he explains that Paul's "tolerance" of cultural difference actually turns out to be intolerant of those for whom the practise of their cultural traditions are at the very core of their identity. Paul actually ends up undermining the social and cultural integrity of the Law observant "Christians," because they are forced to acknowledge the equal validity of *non-observance*. Paul's relativization of cultural differences threatens the very seriousness with which they are taken by their practitioners.[24]

---

24. Here Barclay agrees with Boyarin, in that a dialectic between common values and cultural difference must be maintained, and "somewhere in this dialectic a synthesis must be found, one that will allow for stubborn hanging on to ethnic, cultural specificity but in a context of deeply felt and enacted human solidarity" (1994:257). Barclay actually then goes on to say that Paul's ethic and his creation of cross-cultural communities is already pointing towards such "deeply felt and enacted human solidarity." Ultimately, Paul can be used as a valuable resource to fashion a harmonious but multicultural (and multireligious) society. First, Paul deconstructs his own Christological exclusivism by

So what advantage, then, is there in being a Judean? "Much in every way!," Paul answers. They received the words of God (Rom 3:2; cf. 2:18–20). But is there perhaps more? Esler explains that in the allegory of the olive tree (Rom 11:17–24) non-Israelites, likened to wild branches that cannot produce edible fruit, are represented as grafted into Israel, a cultivated olive tree. Paul wants to promote the status of Israel and take his non-Judean audience down a few notches, and so constructs a picture quite unflattering to non-Judeans. They are attached to the cultivated olive tree in a way that Paul describes as contrary to nature (Rom 11:24). They contribute nothing to it as they will not produce fruit, and are actually "parasitic upon its richness" (Esler 2003b:124). The implication is that contrary to this, if the natural branches were to be grafted back in, they will produce more fruit. What Paul writes here was in response to non-Judean arrogance ("boasting") towards Israel among believers in Rome (cf. Rom 11:13, 18, 20; Esler 2003b:121–22, 124). Esler suggests that Paul spent his career arguing that the Mosaic Law was not necessary for non-Israelites.

> Yet this did not mean that he had forgotten his primary socialization as an Israelite, or that his work with non-Israelites had led him to abandon his pride in his Israelite ethnicity, based on an unshakeable belief that Israel had prior place in God's affections and would one day be restored to its privileges ... [When pushed Paul will] suddenly allow a long submerged aspect of his self to become salient in a passionate expression of his original affiliations of kinship and ethnicity. (Esler 2003b:124)

We can ask, however: Was this Paul pampering Israel, or was this really Paul taking pride in his Israelite ethnicity? Is this Paul merely addressing a particular situation, or a Paul passionately expressing his original yet still relevant affiliation of ethnicity? It boils down to some important questions we need to ask:

1. Is Paul an observer of, or (part-time) participant in Israelite ethnic identity?

---

his pervasive appeal to the grace of God. Second, Paul can be seen as the fashioner of multiethnic and multicultural communities, which do not erase, but moderate between differing cultural phenomena (Barclay 1996:213–14).

What Advantage Is There in Being a Judean?

2. Has Paul, from an Israelite point of view, not merely become a spectator, being an outsider now looking in, and at times, a participant when it suits his purposes?

I have argued elsewhere that Paul has grown out of the Judean way of life and that his new identity communicated inclusivity and an alternative mode of being (cf. Cromhout 2009). If we can speak of Paul the Israelite, that identity has either new content where Gentiles can participate in the "Israel of God" *as Gentiles*, or it is what ethnicity theory describes as "situational," meaning it is an identity activated when the social situation requires it. It is an *optional* identity to be used or not used, no longer being an absolute means of self-identification. But whatever "loss" Paul suffered for the sake of knowing Messiah, he remains to be emotionally attached to the Israelite people and sees in them inherent potential as the "natural branches." There is still a sense of belonging on his part, or differently put, Paul wants ethnic Israel to belong with him to God's newly constituted *ethnos*.

Yet according to Paul, being the natural branches of a cultivated olive tree have even more advantages that Gentiles do not have. In Rom 11:1, 5, Paul spoke of the chosen remnant within Israel, yet the present situation of ethnic Israel as a whole is not final (Rom 11:11–32). From a redemptive-historical perspective, their election still stands: "they are loved on account of the fathers, for God's gifts and his call are irrevocable" (Rom 11:28–29). Romans 11:27 (quoting Isa 59:20, 21) and the context within which it is found assumes that a covenant relationship still exists between God and ethnic Israel, that is why the latter is assured eschatological salvation—"all Israel will be saved" (Rom 11:26; cf. *m. Sanh.* 10:1). The blindness that has come upon Israel is temporary, "until the fullness of the Gentiles has come in" (Rom 11:25).[25] And Paul specifically takes the view that it is *God's* redemptive action, and not Israel's repentance, not the Gentile mission, nor any human agency that will initiate Israel's salvation (Baker 2005:482–83). In Romans 9–11 Paul therefore argues that the success of the Torah-free mission to Gentiles, and the failure of the Israelite

---

25. Here Paul also reverses if not abandons the traditional eschatological scheme. The Gentiles will not gather to Zion as a consequence of Israel being saved. Rather, Israel will be saved after the completion of the Gentile mission (cf. Sanders 1983:195; and the counterview of Donaldson 1993:92). As Donaldson notes, Paul does not cite pilgrimage texts.

mission, does not mean the failure of God's covenantal promises to ethnic Israel. The present situation will be overturned.

> Up to 11:10 Paul has defined Israel solely in terms of the faithful remnant (9:6b-9; 11:1–10); defended God's elective freedom to choose the children of promise from the Gentiles as well as the Jews (9:10–29); and demonstrated the culpability of the remainder of Israel for rejecting the gospel (9:30–10:21) . . . But from 11:11 the argument proceeds on the assumption that only if Paul can establish the eventual salvation of "all Israel" . . . will he be able to affirm that "God has not rejected his people" (cf. 11:1). (Donaldson 1993:89)

Paul's language also appears to suggest that Israel's reversal—presumably through their acceptance of Messiah Jesus—will precede the eschatological age, will trigger the resurrection and coincide with the parousia (11:11-15; Donaldson 1993:93). Romans 9–11 is therefore similar to Deuteronomy 32, where we also find the motifs of Israel's unfaithfulness, provoking Israel to jealousy, and God's near abandonment of Israel (Baker 2005:475–76).

So what advantage is there to being a Judean? In short, according to Paul, it exists as latent potential being part of the "natural branches," and in God's continual affection and commitment to save your people. In terms of the latter, what better advantage exists than that? Israel may indeed "boast" about her salvation-historical privileges after all being a testimony to the extent of divine grace we can find in Paul. Or is it a little too late? What Paul says is that it has nothing to do with what you currently do ("works [of the law]"), your values or way of life, or what you believe to be true, but has everything to do with what you may potentially do or with God's faithfulness and relationship he established with your forefathers (cf. Ezek 33:24; Jer 9:24–25; *T. Levi* 15:4; *L.A.B.* 35:3; 2 Macc 8:15). In the process he undermines, if not entirely wipes off the table, his earlier arguments for equality between Israelite and Gentile, or perhaps, can the divine grace that covers Israel be extended to cover all people? In the end both groups may walk away feeling somewhat empty-handed—that is, if they want to play the comparison game. Alternatively, Paul calls us to exercise humility in the presence of divine intention, where, to paraphrase Paul, all forms of "boasting" are excluded.

What Advantage Is There in Being a Judean?
THE IMPACT OF THE NEW PERSPECTIVE ON PAUL

There have been attempts to argue away the NPP; but if a guess may be ventured here, in the long run attempts will fail. It is simply due to the fact that Dunn and likeminded scholars deal with the realities of human culture and social interaction, the very place where the New Testament was born. The authors wrote for communities addressing realities and social contexts that were different from our own. Their "theology" was one and the same as our "sociology"—to separate these realms of life is anachronistic. Life and a relationship with God were experienced within the context of communities and forming part of the social praxis of a group who was the source of your identity and honor.

Despite the shortcomings of the NPP, it has opened up an essential avenue of interpretation in Pauline studies, helping us to recognize the social and ethnic contexts of Paul's struggle to create one people out of the many. Paul argued against the "works (of the law)" as an activity, and therefore as an exclusive identity, because it encoded a privileged way of life communicated by a particular *ethnos*. It encoded the self-understanding of a people where it was understood that God's salvation, as well as the status of righteousness, were only experienced in its fullness when participating within the Judean way of life. Paul disagreed. As we have argued above, he removes "righteousness" as an inherent quality from Israelite identity in two ways. First, God sends rain on the just and the unjust. Justification is God's exclusive right to give to all human beings through the faithfulness of his Messiah. Second, human beings are invited to participate in new values and a new way of life ("faithfulness")—in other words, to have relationships with God and other human being of a different quality, and so acquire a new identity. It is here where the patron of patrons bestows honor and righteousness.

We also focussed on how Paul's argument against the "works (of the law)" was likely to have been received by Israelites, and how Paul's arguments inherently posed a challenge to the Israelite understanding of being a privileged people. He went contrary to all experience of collectivism, honor and shame, categorization, stereotyping, and intergroup comparison. Such a context could explain a lot why ethnic Israel rejected the gospel. If you walked in Israelite sandals he questioned the truthfulness of your very being and mode of existence, your "knowledge," your group membership and boundary, your relationships to "us" or "them," as well as your honor and sense of worth. He challenged you to look at the "other" with different eyes, as your equals, as also the objects of divine favor and called to share in the kingdom of God and his Messiah. In the agonistic world of Paul this form of "identity death" was a tough ask, although Paul himself could write that "I have been crucified with Messiah and I no longer live, but Messiah lives in me" (Gal 2:19).

When engaging with the writings of Paul, first-century Israel can all too easily be dismissed as ethnocentric when evaluating themselves as "superior" to the "other." But in this respect they were no different from other ethnic groups of their day, even from various groups that exist today. If we are walking in Israelite sandals we will discover a part of ourselves, for we are human too, all too eager to make comparisons, to safeguard our own identities, to build social (and confessional) boundaries, and to think of ourselves as belonging to "the best." Paul's understanding of the gospel should give us enough reason for pause and reflection, for it demonstrates that divine action exposes any human constructions of identity as presumptuous and brittle. In other words, our perspective on the world is nothing other than a self-serving pat on the back. His experience, to the contrary, teaches us that our dignity, sense of worth and identity—including that of the "other"—is ultimately not ours to determine.

Bibliography

Aguilar, Mario I. 2000. "Rethinking the Judean Past: Questions of History and A Social Archaeology of Memory in the First Book of the Maccabees." *BTB* 30:58–67.

Baker, Murray. 2005. "Paul and the Salvation of Israel: Paul's Ministry, the Motif of Jealousy, and Israel's Yes." *CBQ* 67:469–84.

Banks, Marcus. 1996. *Ethnicity: Anthropological Constructions*. London: Routledge.

Barclay, John M. G. 1996. "'Neither Jew Nor Greek': Multiculturalism and the New Perspective on Paul." In *Ethnicity and the Bible*, edited by Mark G. Brett, 197–214. Biblical Interpretation Series 19. Leiden: Brill.

Barth, Fredrik, editor. 1969. *Ethnic Groups and Boundaries*. Scandinavian University Books. Boston: Little, Brown.

———. 1994. "Enduring and Emerging Issues in the Analysis of Ethnicity." In *The Anthropology of Ethnicity: Beyond "Ethnic Groups and Boundaries,"* edited by Hans Vermeulen and Cora Govers, 11–32. Amsterdam: Spinhuis.

Bassler, Jouette M. 1984. "Divine Impartiality in Paul's Letter to the Romans." *NovT* 26:43–58.

Bauer, Walter, et al., editors. 2000. *A Greek-English Lexicon of the New Testament and Other Early Christian Literature*. 3rd ed. Chicago: University of Chicago Press.

Baumgarten, Albert I. 1997. *The Flourishing of Jewish Sects in the Maccabean Era: An Interpretation*. JSJSup 55. Leiden: Brill.

Beker, J. Christiaan. 1986. "The Faithfulness of God and the Priority of Israel in Paul's Letter to the Romans." *HTR* 79:10–16.

Bell, Catherine. 1997. *Ritual: Perspectives and Dimensions*. New York: Oxford University Press.

Bentley, G. Carter. 1987. "Ethnicity and Practice." *Comparative Studies in Society and History* 29:24–55.

———. "Response to Yelvington." *Comparative Studies in Society and History* 33:169–75.

Berger, Peter L. 1973. *The Social Reality of Religion*. Penguin University Series. Harmondsworth, UK: Penguin.

Berger, Peter L., and Thomas Luckmann. 1966. *The Social Construction of Reality: A Treatise in the Sociology of Knowledge*. Garden City, NY: Doubleday.

Bernstein, George. 1984. "Ethnicity: The Search for Characteristics and Context." *Theory into Practice* 23:98–103.

Berry, John W., et al. 2002. *Cross-Cultural Psychology. Research and Applications*. 2nd ed. Cambridge: Cambridge University Press.

Bird, Michael F. 2005. "When the Dust Finally Settles: Coming to a Post–New Perspective Perspective." *CTR* 2:57–69.

———. 2007. *The Saving Righteousness of God: Studies on Paul, Justification and the New Perspective*. Eugene, OR: Wipf & Stock.

Bibliography

Botha, J. Eugene. 2007. "Exploring issues around Biblical, Western, and African Social Values." *HvTSt* 63:147–69.

Bourdieu, Pierre. 1977. *Outline of a Theory of Practice*. Translated by Richard Nice. Cambridge Studies in Social Anthropology 16. Cambridge: Cambridge University Press.

Boyarin, Daniel. 1994. *A Radical Jew: Paul and the Politics of Identity*. Contraversions 1. Berkeley: University of California Press.

Brett, Mark G., editor. 1996. *Ethnicity and the Bible*. Biblical Interpretation Series. 19. Leiden: Brill.

Brewer, Marilynn B. 1999. "The Psychology of Prejudice: Ingroup Love or Outgroup Hate?" *Journal of Social Issues* 55:429–44.

Brown, Rupert. 1995. *Prejudice: Its Social Psychology*. Oxford: Blackwell.

———. 2001. *Group Processes: Dynamics within and between Groups*. 2nd ed. Oxford: Blackwell.

Brubaker, Rogers, et al. 2004. "Ethnicity as Cognition." *Theory and Society* 33:31–64.

Brueggemann, Walter. 2002. *The Land: Place as Gift, Promise, and Challenge in Biblical Faith*. 2nd ed. OBT. Minneapolis: Fortress.

Byrne, Brendan. 2001. "Interpreting Romans Theologically in a Post-'New Perspective' Perspective." *HTR* 94:227–41.

Carson, D. A, et al., editors. 2001. *Justification and Variegated Nomism: A Fresh Appraisal of Paul and Second Temple Judaism*. Vol. 1, *The Complexities of Second Temple Judaism*. WUNT 2/140. Grand Rapids: Baker Academic.

Carter, Warren. 2006. *The Roman Empire and the New Testament: An Essential Guide*. Abingdon Essential Guides. Nashville: Abingdon.

Chance, John K. 1996. "The Anthropology of Honor and Shame: Culture, Values, and Practice." *Semeia* 68:139–51.

Chestnut, Randall D. 2006. "*Joseph and Asenath*: Food as an Identity Marker." In *The Historical Jesus in Context*, edited by Amy-Jill Levine, et al., 357–65. Princeton Readings in Religions. Princeton: Princeton University Press.

Cohen, Shaye J. D. 1987. *From the Maccabees to the Mishnah*. LEC 7. Philadelphia: Westminster.

———. 1993. "'Those Who Say They Are Jews and Are Not': How Do You Know a Jew in Antiquity When You See One?" In *Diasporas in Antiquity*, edited by Shaye J. D. Cohen and Ernest S. Frerichs, 1–45. BJS 288. Atlanta: Scholars.

Craffert, Pieter F. 2007. *The Life of a Galilean Shaman: Jesus of Nazareth in Anthropological-Historical Perspective*. Matrix: The Bible in Mediterranean Context 3. Eugene, OR: Cascade Books.

Cromhout, Markus. 2007. *Jesus and Identity: Reconstructing Judean Ethnicity in Q*. Matrix: The Bible in Mediterranean Context 2. Eugene: Cascade Books.

———. 2009. "Paul's 'Former Conduct in the Judean Way of Life' (Gal 1:13) . . . or Not?" *HvTSt* 2009: 12 pp. Online: http://www.hts.org.za/index.php/HTS/article/view/127/224

Crook, Zeba. 2004. "BTB Readers' Guide: Loyalty." *BTB* 34:167–77.

De Boer, Martinus C. 2005. "Paul's Use and Interpretation of a Justification tradition in Galatians 2.15–21." *JSNT* 28:189–216.

Denzey, Nicola. 2002. "The Limits of Ethnic Categories." In *Handbook of Early Christianity: Social Science Approaches*, edited by Anthony J. Blasi, et al., 489–507. Walnut Creek, CA: AltaMira.

Bibliography

DeSilva, David A. 1996. "The Wisdom of Ben Sira: Honor, Shame, and the Maintenance of Values of a Minority Culture." *CBQ* 58:433–55.

De Vos, George. 1975. "Ethnic Pluralism: Conflict and Accommodation." In *Ethnic Identity: Cultural Continuities and Change*, edited by George De Vos and Lola Romanucci-Ross, 5–41. Palo Alto, CA: Mayfield.

Donaldson, Terence L. 1993. "'Riches for the Gentiles' (Rom 11:12): Israel's Rejection and Paul's Gentile Mission." *JBL* 112:81–98.

Douglas, Mary T. 1966. *Purity and Danger: An Analysis of the Concepts of Pollution and Taboo.* London: Routledge & Kegan Paul.

Duling, Dennis C. 2005. "Ethnicity, Ethnocentrism, and the Matthean *ethnos.*" *BTB* 35:125–43.

———. 2008a. "'Whatever gain I had . . .': Ethnicity and Paul's Self-Identifications in Philippians 3:5–6." *HvTSt* 64:799–818. Online: http://ajol.info/index.php/hts/article/viewFile/41305/8685.

———. 2008b. "2 Corinthians 11:22: Historical Context, Rhetoric, and Ethnicity." *HvTSt* 64:819–43. Online: http://ajol.info/index.php/hts/article/viewFile/41299/8679.

———. 2010. "Ethnicity and Paul's Letter to the Romans." In *Understanding the Social World of the New Testament*, edited by Dietmar Neufeld and Richard DeMaris, 68–89. New York, NY: Routledge.

Dunn, James D. G. 1988. *Romans 9–16*. Word Biblical Commentary 38B. Dallas: Word.

———. 1990. *Jesus, Paul and the Law: Studies in Mark and Galatians.* Louisville: Westminster John Knox.

———. 1991. *The Partings of the Ways between Christianity and Judaism and Their Significance for the Character of Christianity.* Philadelphia: Trinity.

———. 1997. "Once More PISTIS CHRISTOU." In *Looking Back, Pressing On*, edited by E. Elizabeth Johnson and David M. Hay, 61–81. Pauline Theology 4. Atlanta: Scholars.

———. 2003. *Jesus Remembered.* Christianity in the Making 1. Grand Rapids: Eerdmans.

———. 2008. *The New Perspective on Paul.* Rev ed. Grand Rapids: Eerdmans.

Eilberg-Schwartz, Howard. 1990. *The Savage in Judaism: An Anthropology of Israelite Religion and Ancient Judaism.* Bloomington: Indiana University Press.

Eller, Jack David, and Reed M. Coughlan. 1993. "The Poverty of Primordialism: The Demystification of Ethnic Attachments." *ERS* 16:185–202.

Elliott, John H. 1991. "Household and Meals vs. Temple Purity Replication Patterns in Luke-Acts." *BTB* 21:102–9.

———. 2007. "Jesus the Israelite Was Neither a 'Jew' Nor a 'Christian': On Correcting Misleading Nomenclature." *JSHJ* 5:119–54.

Esler, Philip F. 1996. "Group Boundaries and Intergroup Conflict in Galatians: A New Reading of Galatians 5:13—6:10." In *Ethnicity and the Bible*, edited by Mark G Brett, 215–40. Biblical Interpretation Series 19. Leiden: Brill.

———. 1998. *Galatians.* New Testament Readings. London: Routledge.

———. 2000. "The Mediterranean Context of Early Christianity." In *The Early Christian World*, vol. 1, edited by Philip F. Esler, 3–25. London: Routledge.

———. 2003a. *Conflict and Identity in Romans: The Social Setting of Paul's Letter.* Minneapolis: Fortress.

———. 2003b. "Ancient Oleiculture and Ethnic Differentiation: The Meaning of the Olive-Tree Image in Romans 11." *JSNT* 26:103–24.

———. 2003c. "Social Identity, the Virtues, and the Good Life: A New Approach to Romans 12:1—15:13." *BTB* 33:51–63.

Bibliography

———. 2006. "Paul's Contestation of Israel's (Ethnic) Memory of Abraham in Galatians 3." *BTB* 36:23–33.

Fenton, Steve. 2003. *Ethnicity.* Key Concepts. Cambridge: Polity.

Fiensy, David A. 1991. *The Social History of Palestine in the Herodian Period: The Land Is Mine.* SBEC 20. Lewiston, NY: Mellen.

Fishman, Joshua. 1996. "Ethnicity as Being, Doing, and Knowing." In *Ethnicity*, edited by John Hutchinson and Anthony D. Smith, 63–69. Oxfordreaders. Oxford: Oxford University Press.

Frijda, Nico H., and Batja Mesquita. 1994. "The Social Roles and Functions of Emotions." In *Emotion and Culture. Empirical Studies of Mutual Influence*, edited by Shinobu Kitayama and Hazel Rose Markus, 51–88. Washington DC: American Psychological Association.

Garlington, Don. 2005. "The New Perspective on Paul: An Appraisal Two Decades On." *CTR* 2:17–38.

Gathercole, Simon J. 2002. *Where Is Boasting? Early Jewish Soteriology and Paul's Response in Romans 1–5.* Grand Rapids: Eerdmans.

Geertz, Clifford. 1963. "The Integrative Revolution: Primordial Sentiments and Civil Politics in the New States." In *Old Societies and New States: The Quest for Modernity in Asia and Africa*, edited by Clifford Geertz, 105–57. New York: Free Press.

———. [1973] 2000. "The Integrative Revolution: Primordial Sentiments and Civil Politics in the New States." In *The Interpretation of Cultures*, 255–310. New York: Basic Books.

Grosby, Steven. 1996. "The Inexpungeable Tie of Primordiality." In *Ethnicity*, edited by John Hutchinson and Anthony D. Smith, 51–56. Oxfordreaders. Oxford: Oxford University Press.

Gruen, Erich S. 2002. *Heritage and Hellenism: The Reinvention of Jewish Tradition.* Hellenistic Culture and Society 30. Berkeley: University of California Press.

Guijarro, Santiago. 2001. "Kingdom and Family in Conflict: A Contribution to the Study of the Historical Jesus." In *Social Scientific Models for Interpreting the Bible: Essays by the Context Group in Honor of Bruce J. Malina*, edited by John J. Pilch, 210–38. Biblical Interpretation Series 53. Leiden: Brill.

Hall, Jonathan M. 1997. *Ethnic Identity in Greek Antiquity.* Cambridge: Cambridge University Press.

———. 2002. *Hellenicity: Between Ethnicity and Culture.* Chicago: University of Chicago Press.

Hanson, K. C. 1994. "BTB Reader's Guide to Kinship." *BTB* 24:183–94. Online: http://www.kchanson.com/ARTICLES/kinship.html/.

———. 1994[96]. "'How Honorable!' 'How Shameful!' A Cultural Analysis of Matthew's Makarisms and Reproaches." *Semeia* 68:81–111.

———. 1996. "Kinship." In *The Social Sciences and New Testament Interpretation*, edited by Richard L Rohrbaugh, 62–79. Peabody, MA: Hendrickson.

———. 2008. "All in the Family: Kinship in Agrarian Roman Palestine." In *The Social World of the New Testament: Insights and Models*, edited by Jerome H. Neyrey and Eric C. Stewart, 25–46. Peabody, MA: Hendrickson.

Harland, Philip A. 2003. *Associations, Synagogues, and Congregations: Claiming a Place in Ancient Mediterranean Society.* Minneapolis: Fortress.

Hay, David M. 1989. "*PISTIS* as 'Ground for Faith' in Hellenized Judaism and Paul." *JBL* 108:461–76.

Bibliography

Hays, Richard B. 2002. *The Faith of Jesus Christ: The Narrative Substructure of Galatians 3:1—4:11.* 2nd ed. Grand Rapids: Eerdmans.

Hooker, Morna D. 1990. *From Adam to Christ: Essays on Paul.* Cambridge: Cambridge University Press.

Horbury, William. 2006. "Cena Pura and Lord's Supper." In *Herodian Judaism and New Testament Study,* 104–41. WUNT 193. Tübingen: Mohr/Siebeck.

Horowitz, Donald L. 1985. *Ethnic Groups in Conflict.* Berkeley: University of California Press.

Horsley, Richard A. 1987. *Jesus and the Spiral of Violence: Popular Resistance in Roman Palestine.* San Francisco: HarperSanFrancisco. Reprinted, Minneapolis: Fortress, 1993.

———. 1995. "Social Conflict in the Synoptic Sayings Source Q." In *Conflict and Invention: Literary, Rhetorical and Social Studies on the Sayings Gospel Q,* edited by John S. Kloppenborg, 37–52. Valley Forge, PA: Trinity.

Horsley, Richard A., and Jonathan A. Draper. 1999. *Whoever Hears You Hears Me: Prophets, Performance, and Tradition in Q.* Harrisburg, PA: Trinity.

Jacobson, David. 2002. "Herod's Roman Temple." *BAR* 28.2:18–27, 60–61.

Jenkins, Richard. 1994. "Rethinking Ethnicity: Identity, Categorization and Power." *ERS* 17:197–223.

———. 1997. *Rethinking Ethnicity: Arguments and Explorations.* London: Sage.

———. 2003. "Rethinking Ethnicity: Identity, Categorization, and Power." In *Race and Ethnicity: Comparative and Theoretical Approaches,* edited by John Stone and Rutledge Dennis, 59–71. Blackwell Readers in Sociology 11. Malden, MA: Blackwell.

Jewett, Robert. 2003. "Paul, Shame, and Honor." In *Paul in the Greco-Roman World: A Handbook,* edited by J. Paul Sampley, 551–74. Harrisburg, PA: Trinity.

Johnson, Luke T. 1982. "Rom 3:21–26 and the Faith of Jesus." *CBQ* 44:77–90.

Jones, Siân. 1997. *The Archaeology of Ethnicity: Constructing Identities in the Past and Present.* London: Routledge.

Kim, Seyoon. 2001. *Paul and the New Perspective: Second Thoughts on the Origin of Paul's Gospel.* Grand Rapids: Eerdmans.

King, Philip J., and Lawrence E. Stager. 2001. *Life in Biblical Israel.* Library of Ancient Israel. Louisville: Westminster John Knox.

Kloppenborg, John S. 2006. "The Theodotos Synagogue Inscription and the Problem of First-Century Synagogue Buildings." In *Jesus and Archaeology,* edited by James H. Charlesworth, 236–82. Grand Rapids: Eerdmans.

Levine, Hal B. 1999. "Reconstructing Ethnicity." *Journal of the Royal Anthropological Institute* 5:165–80.

Lieu, Judith. 2002. *Neither Jew nor Greek? Constructing Early Christianity.* Studies in the New Testament and Its World. London: T. & T. Clark.

MacDonald, Margaret Y. 1999. "Ritual in Pauline Churches." In *Social-Scientific Approaches to New Testament Interpretation,* edited by David G. Horrell, 233–47. Edinburgh: T. & T. Clark.

Mahmood, Cynthia K., and Sharon L. Armstrong. 1992. "Do Ethnic Groups Exist? A Cognitive Perspective on the Concept of Cultures." *Ethnology* 31:1–14.

Malina, Bruce J. 1993. *The New Testament World: Insights from Cultural Anthropology.* 3rd ed. Louisville: Westminster John Knox.

Bibliography

———. 1996. "Understanding New Testament Persons." In *The Social Sciences and New Testament Interpretation*, edited by Richard L. Rohrbaugh, 41–61. Peabody, MA: Hendrickson.

Malina, Bruce J., and Jerome H. Neyrey. 1996. *Portraits of Paul. An Archaeology of Ancient Personality*. Louisville: Westminster John Knox.

———. 2008. "Ancient Mediterranean Persons in Cultural Perspective: Portrait of Paul." In *The Social World of the New Testament: Insights and Models*, edited by Jerome H. Neyrey and Eric C. Stewart, 257–75. Peabody, MA: Hendrickson.

Malina, Bruce J., and Richard L. Rohrbaugh. 1992. *Social-Science Commentary on the Synoptic Gospels*. Minneapolis: Fortress.

Marohl, Matthew J. 2008. *Joseph's Dilemma: "Honor Killing" in the Birth Narrative of Matthew*. Eugene, OR: Cascade Books.

Martin, J. Louis. 1998. *Galatians: A New Translation with Introduction and Commentary*. AB 33A. New York: Doubleday.

Mason, Steve, with Michael W. Helfield. 2009. *Josephus, Judea, and Christian Origins: Methods and Categories*. Peabody, MA: Hendrickson.

McVann, Mark S. 1993a. "Change/Novelty Orientation." In *Biblical Social Values and Their Meaning: A Handbook*, edited by John J. Pilch and Bruce J. Malina, 17–20. Peabody: Hendrickson.

———. 1993b. "Compliance." In *Biblical Social Values and Their Meaning: A Handbook*, edited by John J. Pilch and Bruce J. Malina, 31–33. Peabody, MA: Hendrickson.

Miller, James C. 2001. "The Romans Debate: 1991–2001." *CR:BS* 9:306–49.

———. 2008. "Ethnicity and the Hebrew Bible: Problems and Prospects." *Currents in Biblical Research* 6:170–213.

Moxnes, Halvor. 1996. "Honor and Shame." In *The Social Sciences and New Testament Interpretation*, edited by Richard L. Rohrbaugh, 19–40. Peabody, MA: Hendrickson.

Neufeld, Dietmar 2000. "Jesus' Eating Transgressions and Social Impropriety in the Gospel of Mark: A Social Scientific Approach." *BTB* 30:15–26.

Neyrey, Jerome H. 1988. "Unclean, Common, Polluted, and Taboo. A Short Reading Guide." *Foundations and Facets Forum* 4,4:72–82.

———. 1990. *Paul, in Other Words. A Cultural Reading of His Letters*. Louisville: Westminster John Knox.

———. 1996. "Clean/Unclean, Pure/Polluted, and Holy/Profane: The Idea and the System of Purity." In *The Social Sciences and New Testament Interpretation*, edited by Richard L Rohrbaugh, 80–106. Peabody, MA: Hendrickson.

———. 2008. "Loss of Wealth, Loss of Family, Loss of Honor: The Cultural Context of the Original Markarisms in Q." In *The Social World of the New Testament: Insights and Models*, edited by Jerome H. Neyrey and Eric C. Stewart, 87–102. Peabody, MA: Hendrickson.

Neyrey, Jerome H., and Richard L. Rohrbaugh. 2008. "'He Must Increase, I Must Decrease' (John 3:30): A Cultural and Social Interpretation." In *The Social World of the New Testament: Insights and Models*, edited by Jerome H. Neyrey and Eric C. Stewart, 237–51. Peabody, MA: Hendrickson.

Oakman, Douglas E. 2008. *Jesus and the Peasants*. Matrix: The Bible in Mediterranean Context 4. Eugene, OR: Cascade Books.

Overman, J. Andrew, et al. 2003. "Discovering Herod's Shrine to Augustus." *BAR* 29.2:40–49, 67–68.

Bibliography

Pilch, John J., and Bruce J Malina, editors. 1993. *Biblical Social Values and Their Meaning: A Handbook*. Peabody: Hendrickson.

Reed, Jonathan L. 1999. "Galileans, 'Israelite Village Communities,' and the Sayings Gospel Q." In *Galilee through the Centuries: Confluence of Cultures*, edited by Eric M. Meyers, 87–108. DJSS 1. Winona Lake, IN: Eisenbrauns.

———. 2000. *Archaeology and the Galilean Jesus: A Re-Examination of the Evidence*. Harrisburg, PA: Trinity.

Rohrbaugh, Richard L. 2007. *The New Testament in Cross-Cultural Perspective*. Matrix: The Bible in Mediterranean Context 1. Eugene, OR: Cascade Books.

Roosens, Eugeen. 1994. "The Primordial Nature of Origins in Migrant Ethnicity." In *The Anthropology of Ethnicity: Beyond "Ethnic Groups and Boundaries,"* edited by Hans Vermeulen and Cora Govers, 81–104. Amsterdam: Spinhuis.

Saldarini, Anthony J. 1994. *Matthew's Christian-Jewish Community*. Chicago Studies in the History of Judaism. Chicago: University of Chicago Press.

Sanders, E. P. 1977. *Paul and Palestinian Judaism: A Comparison of Patterns of Religion*. Philadelphia: Fortress.

———. 1983. *Paul, the Law, and the Jewish People*. Minneapolis: Fortress.

———. 1992. *Judaism: Practice and Belief 63 BCE—66 CE*. Philadelphia: Trinity.

Schmidt, Francis. 2001. *How the Temple Thinks: Identity and Social Cohesion in Ancient Judaism*. Translated by J. Edward Crowley. Biblical Seminar 78. Sheffield: Sheffield Academic.

Scott, George M. 1990. "A Resynthesis of the Primordial and Circumstantial Approaches to Ethnic Group Solidarity: Towards and Explanatory Model." *ERS* 13:147–71.

Shanks, Hershel. 2001. "Is It or Isn't It—A Synagogue?" *BAR* 27.6:51–57.

Shils, Edward A. 1957a. *Center and Periphery: Essays in Macrosociology*. Selected Papers of Edward Shils 2. Chicago: University of Chicago Press.

———. 1957b. "Primordial, Personal, Sacred and Civil Ties." *British Journal of Sociology* 8:130–45.

Sloan, Robert B. 1991. "Paul and the Law: Why the Law Cannot Save." *NovT* 33:35–60.

Smiles, Vincent M. 2002. "The Concept of 'Zeal' in Second-Temple Judaism and Paul's Critique of It in Romans 10:2." *CBQ* 64:282–99.

Smith, Anthony D. 1986. *The Ethnic Origins of Nations*. Oxford: Blackwell.

———. 1994. "The Politics of Culture: Ethnicity and Nationalism." In *Companion Encyclopedia of Anthropology*, edited by Tim Ingold, 706–33. Routledge Reference. London: Routledge.

Stanley, Christopher D. 1996. "'Neither Jew nor Greek': Ethnic Conflict in Graeco-Roman Society." *JSNT* 64:101–24.

Stegemann, Ekkehard W., and Wolfgang Stegemann. 1999. *The Jesus Movement: A Social History of Its First Century*. Translated by O. C. Dean Jr. Minneapolis: Fortress.

Stegemann, Wolfgang. 2006. "The Emergence of God's New People: The Beginnings of Christianity Reconsidered." *HvTSt* 62:23–40.

Suny, Ronald Grigor. 2001. "Constructing Primordialism: Old Histories for New Nations." *The Journal of Modern History* 73:862–96.

Tajfel, Henri. 1978. *Differentiation between Social Groups: Studies in the Social Psychology of Intergroup Relations*. European Monographs in Social Psychology 14. London: Academic Press.

———. 1981. *Human Groups in Social Categories: Studies in Social Psychology*. Cambridge: Cambridge University Press.

Bibliography

Tajfel, Henri, and John C. Turner. 1979. "An Integrative Theory of Intergroup Conflict." In *The Social Psychology of Intergroup Relations*, edited by William G. Austin and Stephen Worchel, 33–47. Monterey, CA: Brooks/Cole.

Taylor, Walter F. 2005. "Reciprocity, Siblings, and Paul: Why Act Ethically?" *LTJ* 39:181–95.

Theissen, Gerd. 1992. *Social Reality and the Early Christians: Theology, Ethics, and the World of the New Testament*. Translated by Margaret Kohl. Minneapolis: Fortress.

Thompson, Michael B. 2002. *The New Perspective on Paul*. Grove Biblical Series 26. Cambridge: Grove Books.

Trebilco, Paul R. 1991. *Jewish Communities in Asia Minor*. SNTSMS 69. Cambridge: Cambridge University Press.

Triandis, Harry C. 1994a. "Major Cultural Syndromes and Emotion." In *Emotion and Culture. Empirical Studies of Mutual Influence*, edited by Shinobu Kitayama and Hazel Rose Markus, 285–306. Washington, DC: American Psychological Association.

———. 1994b. *Culture and Social Behavior*. McGraw Hill Series in Social Psychology. New York: McGraw-Hill.

Turner, Nigel. 1965. *Grammatical Insights into the New Testament*. Edinburgh: T. & T. Clark.

Turner, John C., with Michael J. Hogg, et al. 1987. *Rediscovering the Social Group: A Self-Categorization Theory*. Oxford: Blackwell.

Waters, Guy Prentiss. 2004. *Justification and the New Perspectives on Paul. A Review and Response*. Phillipsburg, NJ: Presbyterian & Reformed Publishing.

Watson, Francis. 2007. *Paul, Judaism, and the Gentiles. Beyond the New Perspective*. Rev. ed. Grand Rapids: Eerdmans.

Westerholm, Stephen. 2004. *Perspectives Old and New on Paul: The "Lutheran" Paul and His Critics*. Grand Rapids: Eerdmans.

Wright, N. T. 1997. *What Saint Paul Really Said: Was Paul of Tarsus the Real Founder of Christianity?* Grand Rapids: Eerdmans.

———. 2005. *Paul: In Fresh Perspective*. Minneapolis: Fortress.

Index of Ancient Documents

OLD TESTAMENT

Genesis

9:26	26
10:31	26
17:1	54
17:2–6	54
17:10–14	58
34	28n14

Exodus

6:12	54n3
6:30	54n3
12:26–27	18
13:14–15	18

Leviticus

1:2	53
1:3	53
1:10	53
4:3	53
4:23	53
4:28	53
4:27–35	56
5:15	53
5:18	53
6:2–7	56
9:3	53
11	50, 53
11:29–38	56
11:41–42	53
12	50
12:1–8	56
13–14	50, 56
15	50
15:1–15	56
15:9	56
15:16–17	56
15:18	56
15:19–23	56
15:25–30	56
16	45
19:19	50
21:1–11	50
21:17–21	53
22:20	53
23	45
23:18	53
26:41	54n3

Numbers

3:13	53
8:17–18	53
11:29	28n14
18:15	53
19	50, 55
25:6–13	28n14

Deuteronomy

6:20–24	18
7:1–4	41
10:16	54n3
11:27–28	47
14	50
14:4–6	53
16	45
22:9	50
22:10	50
22:11	50
32	104
32:43	101

Index of Ancient Documents

Joshua

4:6–7	18
4:21–23	18

1 Kings

18	28n14

Ezra

9–10	41

Nehemiah

9–10	41

Psalms

17:50	101
116:1	101

Isaiah

11:10	101
51:1–2	47
59:20	103
59:21	103

Jeremiah

6:10	54n3
9:24–25	104
9:25	54n3

Ezekiel

33:24	104
44:7	54n3

Daniel

1:1–16	60n4
1:8–16	20
10:3	20

Habakkuk

2:4	93

APOCRYPHA

1 Baruch

3:36—4:4	76
4:1	12

1 Maccabees

1:11–13	19
1:15	23
1:62–63	60n4
2:23–27	28n14
2:50–51	29
2:54	28n14
2:58	28n14
15:33	20

2 Maccabees

4:2	28n14
6:18–21	60n4
7:1	60n4
8:15	83n6, 104
11:25	29

Additions to Esther

14:17	20, 60n4

Judith

8:2	41
9:2–4	28n14
10–12	60n4
10:5	20
12:1–20	20

Sirach

10:19–24	29, 42
24:9	12
24:23	76
24:33	12
36:1–9	61n6
45:17	57
45:23–24	28n14
48:2–3	28n14

Index of Ancient Documents

Tobit
1:9	41
1:10–13	20
3:15–17	41
4:12–13	41
4	18

Wisdom of Solomon
11:9–10	83n8
12:22	83n8
16:9–10	83n8
18:4	12

4 Ezra
5:29	46
6:56–59	46
7:11	46
8:56–58	61n6

PSEUDEPIGRAPHA

1 Enoch
10:21	61n6
90:19	61n6
99:14	29

2 Baruch
41:1–6	61n6

2 Enoch
52:9–10	30

3 Maccabees
1:3	29
3:4–7	60n4
6:9	13
6:12	13

4 Maccabees
5:29	29
8:8	58
9:1–2	29
9:29	29
16:16	29
18:1	29
18:10–19	18
18:12	28n14
18:5	29

Joseph and Asenath
7:1	20
8:5	20

Jubilees
3:31	58
8	44
12:2–5	12n7
12:26	70
15:31	61
15:33–34	58
20:4	42
20:7–9	12n7
21:21	13
21:5	12n7
22:11	61, 77
22:16	14, 59, 60n4
22:18	12n7
22:22	12n7
23:24	12
24:29–30	61n6
26:23	61, 77
30	28n14
30:7–8	41
32:19	77

Letter of Aristeas
128–42	60n4
134–35	12n7
139–42	14, 19
151–52	81

Liber antiquitatum biblicarum
32:7	76
35:3	83, 104

Index of Ancient Documents

Lives of the Prophets
4:16	29

Psalms of Solomon
3:4–16	83n8
7:1–10	83n8
8:27–40	83n8
9:8–11	44
13:4–11	83n8
14:5	43
16:21–31	45
17:15	23
17:24	61n6

Sibylline Oracles
3:30–34	12
3:171	12
3:195	76
3:219	13
3:545–54	12n7
3:573	13
3:584–85	61
3:596–600	12n7
3:616–17	61n6
3:670–72	61n6
3:710–20	61n6
3:772–73	61n6
4:24–30	60n4
4:33–34	12n7
5:276–80	12n7
5:430	12n7
5:484–500	12n7

Testament of Job
1:5	43
2:2—3:3	12n7
5:2	12n7

Testament of Moses
2:8–9	12n7

Testaments of the Twelve Patriarchs

Testament of Asher
7:3	61n6

Testament of Benjamin
9:2	61n6
11:1–3	61n6

Testament of Gad
7:2	61n6

Testament of Dan
5:5	13
5:8	13

Testament of Judah
23:2	13

Testament of Levi
8:14	61n6
15:4	104

Testament of Naphtali
3:1–2	12
8:2–4	61n6

Testament of Simeon
7:2	61n6

DEAD SEA SCROLLS

CD
4.7–12	61n6
5.5–6	80
14.4–6	61n6

1QS
5.20–21, 23–24	82n7
6–7	80

Index of Ancient Documents

6.2–23	60n4
6.13–15	61n6
7.15–20	60n4
8.16–19	60n4

1QSa

2.11–22	60n4

4QMMT	82n7
4Q398	82n7

11QTemple

47.5–14	60n5

RABBINIC WRITINGS

Bereshit Rabbah

25.6	54
46.4	54

Pesikta Rabbati

161a	61n6

MISHNAH

Bikkurim

1.4	75n1

Kelim

1.6–9	53
10.1	57

Nedarim

3.11	54

Pesaḥim

10.4	18

Sanhedrin

10.1	103

TOSEPHTA

Megillah

2.7	53

Sanhedrin

13.2	61n6

BABYLONIAN TALMUD

'Abodah Zarah

3b	61n6
36a–b	60n5

Pesahim

57a	46

Shabbat

17b	60n4

JOSEPHUS

Against Apion

1.60	18
2.148	60n4
2.258	60n4
2.165	57
2.170–73	47
2.175–78	57
2.179–81	47
2.184–87	57
2.195–96	14
2.204	18
2.227–86	76

Jewish Antiquities

4.7	33
4.203–4	32
4.304	57
12.271	28n14
14.41	57
14.185ff.	31

Index of Ancient Documents

Jewish Antiquities (cont.)

14.259–61	32
15.268	58
15.328–30	58
15.363–64	58
15.417	14
17.149–67	59
17.207–8	59
18.30	14
18.55–59	59
20.17	22
20.41	22
20.100	22
20.112	46
20.180–81, 206–7	46

Jewish Wars

1.403–7	58
1.651–55	59
2.7	59
2.169–74	59
2.224–27	46
5.449	46
6.420ff.	46
7.50	22

PHILO

Against Flaccus

7.46	44

The Embassy to Gaius

1.212	14
3.155–59	32
36.281	44

Hypothetica

7.12–13	57

The Life of Moses

2.216	57

On the Creation of the World

128	57

On Drunkeness

20–26	32

On Providence

2.64	44

On the Special Laws

1.70	32
1.221	33
2.62	57
4.150	18

On the Virtues

102–8	22

Questions and Answers on Genesis

3.48	54

GRECO-ROMAN AUTHORS

Apollonius of Molon

De Iudaeis

	60n4

Aristotle

Politics

1327b.1–2	5

Cicero

On Duties

1.53–54	9
1.160	13

Diodorus Siculus

Bibliothetica Historica

40.3.4	60n4

Index of Ancient Documents

Hecataeus of Abdera

Aegyptiaca   60n4

Herodotus

Histories
3.37	11
8.144	25

Juvenal

Satires
6.160	78n6
14.96–106	78n6
14.98	78n6
14.103–4	14

Menander Rhetor

2.369.18–370.5	5

Petronius

Satyricon
102.14	78n3

Fragmenta 37   78n3

Philostratus

Vita Apollonii
5.33	60n4

Plutarch

Quaestiones Conviviales
4.5	78n4

Pompeius Trogus

Historicae Philippae
Book 36	60n4

Strabo

Geography
1.2.34	26

Tacitus

Annals
2.10	25
13.51	77

Germania
28	25

Histories
4.64	26
5.1	8
5.2	60n4, 78n5
5.4	78 n.5

Virgil

Aeneid
1.254–82	77
6.851–53	77

Quintilian

Institutio Oratoria
3.7.10–18	5n2

NEW TESTAMENT

Q 22:28	62
Q 22:30	62

Matthew
15:26	99
25:14–45	94n17

John
1:46	76
7:41	76
7:52	76
16:2	23

Acts
10:28	60n4
10:34	77

Index of Ancient Documents

Acts (cont.)

11:2–3	60n4
11:3	19
21:21	23, 76
21:8	23
21:27–31	14
23:8	22

Romans

1–11	100n23
1–3	90
1:3–4	90
1:5	94
1:16–17	80, 90
1:17	90, 94
2:9–10	90
2:11	90
2:13	86, 96n20
2:14–29	96n21
2:16	97
2:17	91
2:17–20	61, 84
2:18–20	102
2:23	91
2:29	85
3:1	73
3:2	102
3:3	88
3:3	90
3:5	90
3:9–20	86
3:20	73, 82n7
3:20–21	86n11
3:20–22	92
3:21–22	84, 90, 91n14
3:21–26	89, 90
3:21–31	92
3:22	90
3:22	88n13, 90
3:22	88
3:22	90
3:29	90
3:23	73
3:24	89, 91
3:25–26	90
3:25	88, 90
3:26	88
3:27	82n7, 91
3:27–28	92
3:27–28	73, 92n16
3:27—4:25	88n13
3:28	86n11
3:28	82n7, 88n13, 92
3:29–30	90
3:29	90
3:31	86
4	90
4:2	91, 92
4:2	82n7
4:4–5	92n15
4:5	94
4:6	82n7
4:9	94
4:11	90
4:12	94
4:13	84, 91n14, 94
4:16	94
4:24	91
5:2	91
5:3	91
5:6	89
5:8	89
5:9	89
5:12–18	89
5:18–19	94
5:19	89
5:20	86
6:3	95
6:15	86n11
6:16	94
7:4	86n11
7:6	86n11
7:10–12	86
7:12	86
7:14	86
7:22–25	86
8:3	86, 89

Index of Ancient Documents

8:9–11	90	14:1	101
8:13	94	14:1–20	74
8:29	89	14:5–9	101
8:33	90	14:1—15:11	101
9–11	90, 103, 104	14:1—15:13	94
9:6b–9	104	14:2–3	93
9:10–29	104	14:10–12	92
9:11	82n7	14:14	101
9:32	82n7	14:20	101
9:30	94	14:15	89
9:30–32	92n15	15:3	94
9:30—10:21	104	15:7	101
10:2	76	15:9–12	101
10:3	90	15:12	90, 96
10:4	73, 84, 86, 90, 91n14	16:25	97

1 Corinthians

10:5	92n15
10:12	73, 90
11:1	104
11:1	103
11:5	103
11:1–10	103
11:5–6	92n15
11:6	82n7
11:10	104
11:11	104
11:11–15	104
11:11–32	103
11:13	102
11:17–24	102
11:18	102
11:20	102
11:24	102
11:25	103
11:26	103
11:26–32	90
11:27	103
11:28–29	103
11:32	90
12:1	94
12:1—13:10	95
12:1—15:3	95, 99n23
12:10	97
13:8–10	86
13:14	93, 94, 95

1:9	90
1:23	76
1:30	90
1:30–31	91
2:16	89, 94
3:13	94
4:3–5	92
6:11	92
5:7	89
7:19	74, 83n8
8:1	96
8:7	101
8:7–13	96
8:8	74
8:11	89
9:19–21	75, 100
10:14–32	96
10:25	101
11:1	93, 94
11:17–34	96
11:25	75
14:26	96
15:3	89
15:20	89
15:21–22	89
15:56	86n11
15:57	90

Index of Ancient Documents

2 Corinthians

1:20	90
3:6	75
3:7	76, 86
3:14	75, 76
4:6	90
5:10	92, 94
5:16–17	95
5:18–19	90
5:21	90
5:19	90
9:8	94
10–13	98
11–12	91
11:21–22	98
11:22	97
11:23–24	76
12:1	98

Galatians

1:4	89
1:10	85
1:13–14	28n14
2:1	90
2:11–12	60n4, 74
2:12	14
2:12–13	20
2:16	74, 82n7, 83, 88
2:19	106
2:19–21	86n11
2:20	88, 89
2:21	84, 89, 91n14
3:2	82n7
3:5	82n7
3:7	74
3:8	91
3:8	90
3:10	82n7, 86n11
3:13	86n11, 89
3:14	90
3:19	86n11
3:22	88
3:23–24	86n11
3:25	93
3:26–28	95
3:27	95
3:28	74
4:3	76
4:4	90
4:5	86
4:9	86n11
4:10	101
4:25	76
5:1	86n11
5:3	86n11
5:6	74, 94
5:13—6:10	95
5:14	86
5:21	94
5:22ff.	93
6:4	89
6:5	92
6:8	94
6:13–14	91
6:15	74, 95

Ephesians

2:11	31
2:14	53n2
4:22–24	95

Philippians

2:4–5	96
2:5	89, 93, 94
2:8	89
3:2–3	99
3:3	99
3:2–11	92n15
3:3	75
3:3–4	98
3:5–6	97, 98, 99
3:6	28n14
3:7–8	98
3:9	84, 86n11, 88, 90, 91n14, 94, 99

Colossians

3:9–10	95

1 Thessalonians

5:9–10	90
5:10	89

James

2:14–16	93

1 Peter

2:21	93

EARLY FATHERS

Euesebius

Praeparatio evangelica

8.7.12–13	57

Justin

Epitome

1.15	60n4

Index of Subjects

advantages of ethnic Israel, 100–104
agonistic societies/contexts, 10–11

baptism, 95

collectivist societies, 8, 22–23, 33, 93
   Israel as example, 10, 34
   social behaviour in, 13, 22–23
   emotion of shame, 23
constructionism, 14ff., 26
   circumstantialism, 15
   instrumentalism, 15
   situationalism, 15
   as response to primordialism, 26
covenantal nomism, 66
   as ethnic descriptor, 35–36
cultural assimilation versus dissimulation, 31
   of Israelites, 31–32

enculturation, 16ff.
   in Israel, 18–19
endogamy, 41
ethnic conflict / cooperation, 3
   in Romans, 100
ethnicity theory
   and biblical studies, 1ff.
   conflicting approaches, 4
   general model, 7ff.
   practice theory, 17
   proposed socio-cultural model, 62–72
   socio-cultural model (Duling), 36–37

ethnicity
   as cultural differentiation or communication, 21ff., 84, 96–97
   as form of cognition, 11
   as shared meaning, 24ff.
   as social activity, 32–33, 57
   cultural features of, 24
      examples in ancient texts, 25–26
   in antiquity, 6
   in collectivist societies, 8
   internalization of identity, 33
   role of kinship in, 8, 41
ethnicism, 60
ethno-symbolism, 61
ethnographic writings, 4–5

faithfulness, 88ff.
   of God, 88, 104
   of Jesus, 88–89, 90
   as way of life, 92–97

habitus, 16–17, 27
   of Israel, 68–69
Hellenism, 19, 30–31, 58
honor and shame, 42–44, 91
   ascribed honor, 43
   in Paul, 91, 99

kinship, 41
   fictive kinship in Paul, 95–96

limited good, 10–11
loyalty, *see* faithfulness.

Index of Subjects

Maccabean crisis, 19–20, 23

New Perspective on Paul, 78ff.
   reactions to, 80–81

orthopraxy (versus orthodoxy), 21–23, 85, 93–94

patriarchal family, 54–55
patronage and clientage, 44–46, 93–94
Paul, the apostle, 66, 73ff.
   honor as Israelite, 99
   on "boasting," 91
   on own Israelite identity, 97–99, 103
   on the law, 85–86, 100–101
plausibility system, 18, 27
primordialism, 26ff.
   of Israelites, 28ff., 70, 84
progymnasmata, 5
purity/impurity, 49–54, 55–57

righteousness
   as part of Israelite identity, 83–84, 96
   of God, 89–90
ritual immersion, 20–21

self-categorization theory, 9ff.
social categorization, 9, 27, 100

social identity theory, 9ff.
socialization, 16ff.
   in Israel, 18–19
   as categorization, 33
stereotyping, 5–6, 10
   of Gentiles and Israelites, 12–13, 59
symbolic universe, 38ff.
   "core values" and "institutions" of Israel, 66–71
   legitimation, 46–48, 67
   maintenance by "experts," 61–62, 71
   of Israel, 41–72
   of Paul, 87ff.
   past, present and future, 48–49
   Paul's challenge, 73ff.
   protection of, 55–61
   order of universe, 49–55
synagoge, role of, 57–58
synergism versus monergism, 80, 93

temple complex (in Jerusalem), 51–53

Western versus African worldviews, 38–40
"works (of the law)," 81–86, 90, 92–93, 96

www.ingramcontent.com/pod-product-compliance
Lightning Source LLC
Chambersburg PA
CBHW031503160426
43195CB00010BB/1095